They Heard What They Thought He Meant

Commentary on the Book of Acts

Glenn Vellekamp

authorHOUSE®

AuthorHouse™
1663 Liberty Drive
Bloomington, IN 47403
www.authorhouse.com
Phone: 1 (800) 839-8640

Published by AuthorHouse 05/05/2016

ISBN: 978-1-5246-0800-2 (sc)
ISBN: 978-1-5246-0801-9 (e)

Preface

I SUPPOSE THE TITLE OF this book suggests different things to different people. One is that the Apostles may not have always heard what Jesus meant but sometimes only what they thought he meant. That is probably the closest assumption that we're making with this commentary. Like all commentaries, it seems like work. First you have to read the book of Acts to have a text in which to refer. Then the different versions. Ugh, the different translations! A friend of mine said, "You used the King James Version didn't you"? Others want newer versions and paraphrases and just something to make it easier to read. There's the NKJV, NLT, NIV, Message, ESV and so on. I've used the original Greek to English by Jay P. Green for 99% of this commentary. It's just easier. Sometimes it's not the choice I would use for the meaning of a word but you can see the different meanings by looking up the word by number in the Strong's concordance/dictionary. Yes, seems like work. But it's like teaching my grandson to print his letters right the first time. He rushes through to finish his homework but it's so sloppy he has to do it over again. Imagine if we got Jesus' message right the first time. We've been influenced. We've all had teachers teach us different things. One thing about the original language is, there's less chance of many interpretations. I told my grandson and I think it applies here, "If you don't have time to do it right the first time, what makes you think you have time to do it over again"? But then how do we know it is right? Well, it's closer to right, being original language; and you don't have to know Greek. It is literally translated word for word. There's still room to make different assumptions but at least they're all based on the same text and within the same context.

There is a saying, "I know you believe you understood what you think I said but I'm not sure you realize that what you heard is not what I meant". Now, that could apply to many of our every day conversations with moms and kids, spouses, employees, all kinds of relationships, and I think it applies here too. They did and wrote what they thought Jesus meant. But then there's the "Perfect Word of God" concern. May I suggest that first we read the book of Acts as an account of Luke's idea of what was going on and see if the assumptions they made line up with Jesus' character. The account of Acts will help us apply Jesus' character to our culture in the 21st century, by learning how they applied it to their culture in the first century. There is only one way to know Jesus' character, that is by reading what he said. Jesus' words are spirit and life. Heaven and Earth may pass away but his words will never pass away. We're counting on that.

Most of us are not Greek or Hebrew scholars and even if we were, we could still miss what Jesus was saying. We need to meditate on not only what is written that he said but hear his voice. A colleague once told me, "I am at a single roadblock. My struggle is every single lexicon and text and interlinear translates "that one word" in the first person and the Greek verb conjugation is pretty clear. This is especially important as I can make every good argument from culture, history, location and more that the context is clear as you point it out." Sometimes in the black and white, what people other than Jesus have said, is not translated according to context and should be. Jesus' words are never contradictory. Jesus' words are the words of God, no one else can or does make that claim. Hear him! By reading this book and of course all the words of Jesus you will be able to know what you believe and why. And although not everyone will agree with you, they will respect your view. It's easy to get sidetracked and lose focus of the gospel. The disciples were ready to "forbid" the one who was casting out demons on Jesus name, simply because he wasn't following with them. Jesus said, "DO NOT FORBID" (Lk 9:49). Just because we may not follow your doctrine or your way of doing things doesn't make us heretics, and vice versa. The litmus test is "does it agree with Jesus' words and character"? Paul said that even if he were to preach another gospel than that of Christ let him be accursed (Gal 1:8). Now that's strong language but the point is the gospel must agree with Christ not Paul or Apollos or Cephas (1 Cor 1:11-13). Surely, all the other denominations other than ours are not heretics. There are two books that will help us in this journey that I recommend to every Bible student; *Victory Over the Darkness*, by Neil T. Anderson and *A View Worth Teaching*, by yours truly under the pen name of Tim Tyler. But for now let's try to read Acts in it's original language or tongue without preconceived ideas about certain words that have been hijacked to only mean certain things to certain denominations. Like "tongues".

Acts 1

I HAVE NOT TAKEN THE time to include the writings of the book of Acts in this book so it is going to be absolutely necessary that you read the chapters in the Bible as we discuss them in this writing. This is by no means a complete analysis of the book of Acts but more of an outline, a conversation starter that could lead to many other discussions about the many topics in this first account of "The Church". Luke begins with referring to the gospel of Luke, so certain things are implied. Among them, words like gospel, church, apostles and the kingdom of God. Nowhere do we have concrete proof that Luke wrote the gospel of Luke but it does seem like he wrote this account. And since he refers to the first word that he wrote, "to Theophilus", we all, for the most part agree it was Luke who wrote Luke. We will see later that arguing over who wrote what really doesn't have anything to do with the value of Jesus' words. We still don't know who wrote "Hebrews"; does it matter? So we'll just go with the titles of the implied authors the books have. Interestingly, he uses the Greek word "logos" when referring to his first account. It means word but can also mean "The Word" as in the gospel of John. Words, whether in Greek, Hebrew or English can have different meanings depending on its use in the sentence or context. (Often in the Strongest Strong's Concordance it says "note the many contextual translations" and in another place, pg xv, referring to compound words it says....."These studies should be done carefully with more attention paid to contextual definitions than

1

fanciful etymologies"). Which is another way of saying, words should support the whole thought of the whole conversation than just standing by themselves in a dictionary. Here, the word "logos" just means the previous writing. In John it means the ultimate word, the final word, the beginning and the ending. We're not sure if Theophilus is one person or as the definition of this word "God lover" implies, any person who loves God. As Luke remembers and as he has been told by eyewitnesses, i.e. the apostles, he writes interchangeably what he experienced and what they witnessed to make one document.

By this time, approximately thirty to forty years after Jesus ascended into heaven, Dr. Luke M.D. came to the realization, like the apostles that Jesus might not be coming back anytime soon. They thought he said," soon", but the original language was the word for "quickly". Jesus said he would come back quickly, (Rev. 22:20, 5035 Strong's; which could mean soon or quickly). Jesus could have meant that when he comes back it will be quickly, like a thief in the night, and not soon. Maybe thousands of years from now, but quickly, like the twinkling of an eye, like lightning. We will be tossing out ideas and different ways of thinking about what was said in an effort to allow us to think differently and be open to what Jesus meant.

There is a song, *The Unshakable Kingdom*, recorded by Sandi Patty. One line in that song seems to sum up what goes on much of the time when we read Jesus' words. The line says, "And in their discontent, they heard what they thought he meant". Unless we think differently, we won't think differently about the things we don't understand. One of those things is "Why hasn't Jesus come back yet?" No wonder "The last days" and "The end times" is always such a best seller. It seems as elusive as trying to lose weight, which is also always a best seller. The point isn't to figure out when he's coming back.......it's to live as he gave us power to live until he does come back. This is what Luke's second account is all about. It's about the "church". Now there's a word with ten thousand meanings.

Everyone who goes to a "church" or has "church" or is the "church" has a different experience and no wonder there are thousands of fragments of the "Church" we call "denominations", which only means "to name". To name what though? A denominator in math divides. And "churches" are divided. This started in Paul's day and he condemned it saying, "Is Christ divided?" (1 Cor.1:13) So when we say "Church" what are we meaning? Many things to many people. I would like to refer to the "Church" as saints who are born from above, who bear fruit of the Spirit, because they are born of the Spirit, those who follow Christ's example. They may go to a building once a week called a "church" or not. They may believe in Calvinism or not. They may be Messianic or not. I believe that the "Church" is the body of Christ not of Paul, not of Cephas, not of Apollos, not Calvin nor Luther. There's nothing wrong with the "Church". The "Church" is working as it should. It's just that the institution that's called the "church", the divided, political, business for profit is not the body of Christ. (Strong's 1577 says church is a group of people, ekklesia, an assembly, never a building or meeting place or a business conglomerate with its own country in Rome, nor a division thereof. All denominations come from the Roman Catholic "church".) Used over 100 times in the Bible, church never means meeting place. It can be old covenant believers or new, but usually new. The Church works. The new testament Church is clean, cleansed by the death and resurrection of Jesus, the expressed image of the invisible God. We say cleansed by "blood" but what we mean is the blood of Jesus, the (Passover) Lamb of God, was emptied out of his body signifying his death. (reading *A View Worth Teaching* by this same author under the pen name of Tim Tyler will help understand some of these ideas).

Those who are truly "born" from above, born of the Spirit, are thankful, gracious people who bear fruit of the Spirit, who love God and love one another as they were loved by Jesus. This is the "Church". There are remnants of the Church in many places, especially in meeting places called churches, because they seek like-mindedness. However, the majority of those who call themselves "Christian" or "The Church" are not. "How can you say that? How do you know? What gives you the right to judge?" I know, I've heard that. But Jesus said, "Few are those who find this way of life." That means few, not many. This means the minority. I think there are many seekers coming to churches seeking to become Christian and there are also many who are just religious. There will be MANY who will say "Lord" but they are not the Church. (Mt 7:14 and 21-23). These are those who imagine that God has the bigger stick and can punish them for not doing, or performing all the right traditions. They don't know him as Savior. If they were asked why they should "inherit" eternal life they would list all the things they did, not that they deserved hell and Jesus paid for their punishment.

The Church has been judged wrongly; imagine that. Imposters, those who are "Christian" in name only have taken the spotlight and have misrepresented the "Church". We don't need to be more like the world to reach lost souls. We, the Church, need to be who we are. Preaching the gospel and using words sometimes, is what works for reaching lost souls. People want to be loved and accepted. That's what works. That's what Jesus came for; that's what he did. He provided a way to be accepted. God loves every human being, but only accepts the forgiven. He gave us all forgiveness freely in the new testament. Everyone. But for some reason most don't accept the forgiveness. I was one of those. It was hard to let someone else pay for my forgiveness. I felt guilty and wanted to pay for forgiveness myself. Even after I received forgiveness, I wanted to pay God back for what he did for me. At age 47 after being "saved" for 23 years I figured out that you can't pay God back for forgiveness and I was able to accept grace, freely, without debt. There is freedom and then there is walking in freedom. It is our calling to make his love and acceptance clear. It's our calling to be ministers of reconciliation. Everyone is forgiven, but not everyone is reconciled. Forgiveness only requires the forgiver. Reconciliation requires both the forgiver and the forgiven. You can forgive a dead person for the hurt they caused you and that helps you, releases you, from past wounds, hurt and anger but it does nothing for the other person. You can't reconcile with a dead person. But we can reconcile with the living. In order for the forgiven by God to be free, he must reconcile with God, (not with people; reconciling with people will help our human relationships but our freedom doesn't depend on it. It depends on being reconciled with God). When forgiveness is offered to the one who caused hurt and pain, he has a choice to reconcile or not. Some respond with "I'm sorry", some respond with "That's just the way I am" or "That's just the way things were back then" or "I'm only human" or "I'm sorry you feel that way". Only "I'm sorry" will lead to reconciliation. It is godly sorrow that leads to repentance. God provides the way of escape from judgment. God gives us forgiveness. But not everyone receives it. Why not? Perhaps they don't understand what forgiveness is. Perhaps they don't understand that you only receive it; you can't earn it or qualify for it or repent for it or be baptized for it. Perhaps we haven't clearly explained it, or more importantly modeled it. It is the gospel. It is the good news. You are forgiven! That's all. That's all; you've been forgiven; you're free. You don't owe me anything; it's over; it's finished; there's no more judgment. Jesus is saying, I have taken all your punishment for all of your wrongdoing past, present and future. Now, how do you respond? It is our response that shows whether we received forgiveness or not. Fruit. A forgiven tree bears forgiven fruit. Love. He who has been forgiven, loves. Being a Christian, becoming part of the Church is reconciliation with God, not just forgiveness from him. We talk about forgiveness in all of our books because I believe it is the single most misunderstood concept in all of Christianity. Without forgiveness and reconciliation there is no Christianity. Without the death and resurrection of Jesus there is no forgiveness nor reconciliation with God. That's why what Mary of Bethany did was so important. She believed in the resurrection before it happened and anointed Jesus for burial believing he would raise from the dead. (and this should be spoken about every time the gospel is preached in the whole world! Mt 26:13) (Read *The Samaritan Woman you never knew*, by this same author).

The account of the acts of the apostles as told by Luke is about reconciliation. It is about the gospel. It is about the church. It is about the ones he "sent" (apostles), reaching lost souls. It is the kingdom of God, the unshakable kingdom of God. But they heard what they thought he meant. They thought there were conditions and requirements. And some think that the account called "Acts" is a pre-scription rather than a de-scription. We, the mixed multitude of saints and sinners, of saved and unsaved, the true Church and Christian in name only, the body of Christ and the institution called "church" have concocted rules and regulations to be "right with God" so that we can be with him when we die. What a mess! The gospel is for now! "You are forgiven", is an invitation to life and life abundantly, NOW! In the Spirit, not, NOT, the cares of this life. Freedom. But it always leads to reconciliation. The forgiven must realize that he is forgiven by the Creator of the universe and receive it. Not what can I do to be saved. It's more like, "What has he done to buy my freedom? I'm so grateful that I want to tell others about this great news! I want to help others to connect and stay connected." This is grace. We are saved by grace. And the grace of God will never lead to sin.

If you think you're forgiven and this justifies you sinning more that grace would be greater, you've missed it. The grace of God teaches us to live godly. We may never be sinless but we should sin less. Should in the sense that it follows. (If the word "should" is used for anything that doesn't naturally follow, then it has judgment written all over it.) Becoming "holy" or sanctification, or renewing the mind, is what naturally follows to one who is reconciled. To the one who has received forgiveness and is born from above, growth in love naturally follows. We can't help but love one another as he loved us......if we realize he loved us. This is the great commission. This is the gospel. This is the Church. This is the kingdom of God, and it is within you. It all hinges on Jesus being raised from the dead, not on our dead works. He's alive! And because he is alive, we can live. This is what "Acts" is all about. As we sift through the minds of the apostles and Luke, let's look for the gospel, the gospel of the kingdom of God.

The apostles were left with a commission that hadn't been done before. Jesus, from the beginning of his ministry said, "Metanoia", being translated" repent", but meaning in the original tongue or language, "Change your thinking", for the kingdom of heaven has drawn near" (Mt.4:17). However, Jesus was the only person in the new testament, the only person in the kingdom of heaven, and he was near. He taught his disciples how to live in the old testament (covenant) using kingdom of heaven (kingdom of God) principles. Now, the disciples were confronted with how to use kingdom of God principles in the new testament. They needed help. They needed power. They needed to receive the Spirit that Jesus had breathed on them, which they hadn't received yet (Jn 20:22).

Jesus had predicted this when he said, "The Spirit of Truth is WITH you, but will be IN you; I am coming to you" (Jn 14:17-18). Jesus gave instructions to them about what to do, to receive the power of the Spirit, to be able to spread the news that he has risen. The women didn't seem to have a problem spreading the news, but they needed power also......nobody believed them. Well, the men didn't believe them. Jesus was seen by them numerous times during the forty days after his resurrection. Paul says in his letter to the Corinthian Church that Jesus was seen by over five hundred believers at one time. There were many convincing proofs. During this same forty day period, the time between Passover and ten days before Pentecost (Shavuot) Jesus was "still" speaking things concerning the "kingdom of God". Not the Kingdom of Israel. Jesus spoke of the invisible kingdom, the kingdom of heaven, the kingdom of God, the kingdom that would never end, the kingdom NOT of this world. But they weren't listening. They were hearing what they thought he meant. We would do well to follow Jesus' words but not necessarily the apostles words because although they were sincere, they misinterpreted the words Jesus spoke. For example, "Will you restore the kingdom to Israel now?" To this day Israel hasn't returned to its former glory. Jesus wasn't interested in the kingdom without, it was the kingdom within you. Jesus wasn't interested in externals but that which is internal that brings results in the external. "Cleanse the inside of the cup and the outside will be cleansed". Just cleansing the outside doesn't last. If the outside hasn't been cleansed, it's because the inside wasn't cleansed first. The new testament is an inside job that bears fruit on the outside. We have only the example of Jesus for this until Pentecost. The Spirit was "with" the apostles but not "in" them......yet. Jesus said, "Wait for it, John baptized in water.......(but you will not be baptized in water, they didn't get that part, to this day we don't get that part; there is one baptism, in the Spirit) but you will be baptized in the Spirit!" (verse 5). You will be immersed in the Spirit! Then the spirit will be "in" you. Then things will change. You will live differently; you will speak differently; I will come to you; I will be "in" you. My body won't be around anymore......you will be my body. The church is the BODY of Christ. We are his offspring, children. God is mother and father and we

7

are children, sons and daughters, inheriting the kingdom, the spiritual kingdom, the kingdom of God. This has always been God's purpose: to bring forth sons and daughters. "The whole creation is groaning and expecting this, namely the revelation of the sons and daughters of God (Rom 8:19, all). Some think that the church is the bride of Christ. A look at Revelation 21 will tell us what the "bride of Christ" is. We are the children of the bride chamber (Mt 9:15).

You will be my witnesses. When the Holy Spirit comes upon you, you will receive power, power to witness about the resurrection to the world! Many have spoken about "the Power" in many places at many times. There are whole "ministries" that promote "Power". There's man-power, woman-power, power to gain wealth, power to heal, power to raise the dead, "spiritual" gifts power, power to speak in a language that no one understands, power to build mega churches. The power that the Holy Spirit gives is the power to" witness". This word in the original language, Greek, is "martyr". The apostles witnessed the resurrection of Jesus. The apostles filled the world with witnessing about the resurrection of Jesus. They witnessed to the death about the resurrection of Jesus. The word for witness, martyr, became synonymous with death for what you believe. They considered it an honor to die for their witness. They considered it an honor to be beaten for their witness. And the more they were persecuted the stronger "the church" got. Today it is reversed. Muslims consider it an honor to die for their cause. They believe they get 70 virgins in the next life if they die for the cause; so threatening them with death only feeds the movement, like early Christianity. Most who call themselves "Christians" today fight for their rights and file lawsuits if they are persecuted and unlike the early "church" are attached to this life and possessions. The apostles witnessed about the resurrection of Jesus because that was the most important thing that happened in their lives. Because he lives again, we live. Nothing else would matter if Jesus was not raised from the dead. We would still be in our sins. Because he rose from the dead we can live without sin, shame, guilt, condemnation, loneliness, depression, deception..........a clean slate. Of course, in the Spirit realm.

Our minds need to grow into this revelation, but at least we have a clear beginning. We are loved and accepted by the holiest one, the Creator of the universes. We start there. We're not trying to get there. We start there. The apostles' physical lives were taken but they live forever. We will notice that everything the apostles said and did hinged on the resurrection and they spoke about it often. From the start of this "account" by Luke it is a continuation of the first account "concerning all things Jesus began both to do and to teach." We would do well to teach what we do. That is if what we are doing is Spiritual. It's not practice what you preach; it's preach what you practice. So many speakers, preachers, try to act humble by self deprecation. They say things like "I'm just a filthy sinner; I still lie and cheat and treat people badly but I'm forgiven." This is not humility. Paul said to "glory in my weaknesses", not my sin. Then they tell us to stop lying and cheating and give advice on marriage and family. This is confusing, words with no power, holding the form and denying the power that Jesus gives us. He gives us power to change and then to witness about that change. It's not true that "we're no different than the world, we're just forgiven and they're not". Without change we are NOT witnesses. If you are still committing adultery, then change. If you can't change then get saved. We are saved by grace, and grace never leads us to sin. If we continue to sin, then we haven't received grace, just religion, superstition and tradition. Do and teach. We should teach what we are doing. That's what Jesus did. If we're not pleased with what we are doing then we should change. Jesus said about the Pharisees, "Do what they say, but don't do as they do". We are Pharisees if we tell others to do what we say but we're not doing it ourselves. To say, "I'm weak but He is strong" doesn't mean I still do all the same sins I did before I got "saved". Glorying in weakness is admitting that, for example, "I don't speak well" or "I'm not the smartest person" or "I realize my physique is not the picture of body building". But to say, "I confess that I'm so smart that I hurt people" is glorying in sin not weakness, or "I'm so attractive I can't help but commit adultery because women chase me", is pride not humility. Humility is confidence properly placed, confidence that Jesus is changing me from the inside, not the public confession of sin.

Some still glory in their past sins, such as, "God delivered me from running the biggest and best prostitution ring in this state", in other words "I was clever and smart and rich and a great businessman (and still am and proud of it) ". Preach what you practice. That's where the power is. "Well, if that's the case, I won't have a whole lot to say. Ok. Less talk more action.

And as he was taken up and a cloud received him, the angels said he would come back the same way and the angels wondered, "Why are you staring into space? This same Jesus will come in the same way you saw him going, (alive, the same physical body, the man, Christ Jesus)". In verse 3, "he presented himself living...... being seen by them". They were eye witnesses (1 Jn 1: 1-4). In other words, "Go witness". But they weren't equipped yet. They hadn't received the Spirit yet. They went to the upper room and waited, the apostles, the disciples, the women and Mary, the mother of Jesus, about 120.

Peter stands up and addresses the men. He decides that since one of the original men, Judas Iscariot, hung himself, we need to replace him so let's draw straws. They picked Matthias. Never heard of him again. Should we follow this example for picking leaders? Is this a prescription for "the Church"? No. It's only a description of what Peter thought should be done before he realized that the" Rock" that Jesus was building his church on was Jesus, himself, not Peter.

Acts 2

THEN ON THE ISRAELITE feast of Shavuot (Pentecost, fifty, (pente) days after another Israelite feast day, First Fruits (resurrection day) which was three days after Passover another Israelite feast, during the seven days of unleavened bread, another feast of the Lord (see a pattern?), the Spirit baptized them. They were immersed in the Spirit and a "sound" from heaven filled the house. IT was a sound. IT sounded like a violent wind. At the same time what appeared to be tongues (something that looked like a human tongue) "as" or resembling fire were dispersed". We speak with our tongues. As a matter of fact we even call languages tongues as in speaking in our native language or "mother tongue". In this writing, Luke always refers to tongue (glossa, 1100 Strong's) as that part of human anatomy or language. Always. In this case the apostles "saw" (probably a vision) something bright that resembled the shape of tongues (that part of human anatomy that represents speaking), the part James spoke about, and they were separate. "As of fire", it was bright, it was a vision from God! I believe what God was showing them was that although men's languages were confounded at the tower of Babel, God was doing something new now; He, God, a consuming fire, the Holy Spirit, was making languages clear, intelligent, understandable and their ability to witness would be supernaturally powered. He would give them power to witness. And IT (the Spirit, with a sound from heaven, like the wind -pneuma) and the tongue shaped lights were placed on each one of them. They were immersed in the Spirit that gave them power, supernatural power to speak about the resurrection of Jesus. They were full of the Holy Spirit and they spoke. They spoke in other languages as the Spirit gave them ability to speak. The Jews from every nation, who spoke in different languages, the "sound" occurring, heard each one speaking in his own language. They wondered, "How?" "They're all Galileans, how do we hear in our own language?" We hear them speaking the great deeds of God in our own language. They were amazed! They were puzzled. They were in wonder! They appeared disoriented or drunk. Others said, "Oh, they're drunk". They who? Which "They"? They that were amazed, puzzled, disoriented. Peter stood up and said, "They (not we) are not drunk as you suppose, it's only 9am". Again Peter, like the "drawing of straws" tries to figure this out. "This is that spoken by the prophet Joel." Well, okay, maybe. Or maybe not. I mean yes, they saw a vision. They spoke (prophesied), and Joel does say that but Joel doesn't say anything about the languages, and that's a giant part of it. And where's all the blood and fire and smoke and darkness? I know Peter is trying to make sense of all this but it might be a stretch to say it's "the last days". After all that was 2000 years ago. Remember they thought Jesus was coming back "soon" not "quickly". Jesus had said, "quickly", maybe thousands of years from now but when he comes it will be "like a thief in the night", "like lightning"......quickly. This is a real hard one to swallow. Since I've been saved I've been looking for the "Second Coming" and all the books! The movies! It's so exciting! But here I am, forty-three years later and we're still waiting. They thought Jesus was returning any day (or night). I did too. That's why I went to Mt Sion, which is Hermon in Israel at midnight on the Feast of Sukkot in 1988 to meet Jesus. I was sold on the idea of the last days! But God. He has a way of causing us to get our focus on the Spirit and not the hype of the day. Jesus didn't return when I thought he would and I learned to witness about his resurrection, back on track.

That's why none of this, what we call the "new testament" was written until 30 or 40 years later. That's when they began to think, "We could die before he comes back, we better write this down." So, the last days? Days? It's been 2000 years, that's a lot of days to be the last (about 730,000 days). So probably not the last days. It's still a popular best seller though. "The End Times", "The Last Days", the rapture, the man of sin, the tribulation, the prophetic, end time prophecy, these are all catchy subjects and catch away (rapture) a lot of people's minds, but I don't think that is what the Spirit was urging them to preach. I think we are supposed to witness about the resurrection of Jesus.... Christ crucified and raised. And that's what they did, Acts 2:24, "but, God raised him up". Now we're back on track, Peter. But oh, so sad that some still think the whole "last days" thing was a prescription of what we're supposed to be preaching. No straws. No Temple. No last days. Jesus, crucified and raised! I've heard on the radio by some well intentioned but misinformed preacher, "You should act like you would if you knew Jesus was coming back tomorrow, what would you do differently if you were warned that he was coming back tomorrow?" That's not the point. We should be witnessing about what he's done not what he's going to do. We should be testifying.... testifying about how his sacrifice has brought change in our lives and power to keep changing. And that, in any language or "tongue", can be understood! Peter is saying now he recognizes that Jesus Christ is a man (2:22). Jesus from Nazareth, a man from God. God did things, miracles, signs, wonders, healings through him. This is still only ten days or so from Jesus ascending. No one knew that Jesus wasn't Joseph's son, except Mary (and Joseph, but he is never mentioned again; he might have died, we don't know). Peter quotes David, says he's a prophet and that he wrote about Jesus. He says that David wrote about the death and resurrection of Jesus. David wrote about the Messiah, and now Peter is saying that Jesus is the Messiah. Something has changed in Peter. No more doubt, fear, disillusionment, denial, shame, guilt and condemnation. He has witnessed the resurrected Messiah and has been given and received power to witness. We have been given the same power to witness. What holds us back?... maybe guilt, shame or condemnation. Maybe we don't know the Bible like we could. Maybe we haven't "received" power. Maybe we're not listening. Read the red words first, always. They are Spirit and they are Life (Jn 6:63)

Peter is now focused on the resurrection. He is focused on Jesus being both Lord and Christ. He quotes the same passage Jesus quoted, "the Lord said to my Lord". Jesus had said, "How can he be both Lord and son?" Peter is saying both Lord and Christ. Peter, still not knowing that Jesus wasn't Joseph's son, has seen the resurrected Jesus and received power to witness and that's enough. No one was required to believe in the "virgin birth" to be "saved", to become part of the "church", not for at least 30 or 40 more years. Why is it required now? Not sure. I believe it. I believe that Jesus was not the son of Joseph nor Mary. I believe that Jesus is the son of God. His body being made in heaven, reduced to a single cell and put into Mary's body as a surrogate mother. I don't believe Mary was without sin. (this is what Roman Catholics commonly refer to as the "immaculate conception", Mary's birth) I believe Jesus was the only sinless man made in heaven, in the "likeness" of sinful flesh, not "in" sinful flesh (Rom 8:3). I believe Jesus is the beginning of the creation of God (Rev 3:14). I believe Jesus is the IMAGE of the invisible God, the firstborn of all creation, all things created through him. I believe he is pre-eminent in all things, including his words, red words (Col 1:15ff, 1 Tim 6:3). I believe that in the days after Jesus began to preach, referred to as "these last days", by the author of Hebrews, God speaks only through his Son (Heb 1:1, Mt 17: 5).

The first thing God created was a body to create everything else through (Heb 10: 7, Col 1:15-16). Mary was created through him. Adam was created through him. Christ's DNA came from heaven; everyone else's came from earth. Adam was formed out of the earth and is earthy, and Satan was already on Earth (so evil was present); the second man is the Lord out of heaven (where no evil is present) (1 Cor 15: 47). We will one day bear the image of the heavenly when our bodies are changed in the twinkling of an eye and we become immortal. Christ's immortal body was from heaven, but being born of a woman caused it to be mortal until the resurrection. But all the appearances of "God" in a body, Melchizedek (without father, without mother, Heb 7:3), The Angel of the Lord, The Captain of the Lord's host, face to face with Moses were in his immortal body. He became mortal to die for us (Phi'p 2:8-11). In Mary, God planted one cell from the immortal body he made in the beginning and it became mortal and grew and was born of a woman. It contained no DNA from Joseph nor Mary and consequently none from David nor Adam. Jesus was not the son of David according to the flesh (Paul didn't know this, Rom 1:3, no one knew until thirty years later when Matthew and Luke shared what Mary told them). He was, however, born into the family of Joseph and legally a son of Joseph and consequently the "son of David", legally. So Peter gets it right, quoting David, because he is focused on the resurrection. Jesus also quoted David when he brought up the issue of the birth of the Christ (Matt 22:41). Jesus questioned the Pharisees saying, "What do you think about the Christ? Whose son is he?" They said to him, "David's". Jesus said to them, "Then how does David in Spirit call him Lord, saying, "The Lord said to my Lord, sit on my right hand until I place your enemies as a footstool for your feet"? Then if David calls him Lord, how is he his son?" NO ONE could answer. No one knew about the virgin birth. They ALL thought Jesus was the son of Joseph and that the Messiah would be the son of David according to the flesh. Those that loved him and those that hated him all thought that he was the son of Joseph. There was no scandal about Jesus being illegitimate. That's just emotional hype for Christmas stories. Peter doesn't know about the birth but he knows about the resurrection. That's where the focus should be. "But Christmas is the most wonderful time of the year". Christmas wasn't conjured up until 300 years later! It's not in the Bible, anywhere. The only time "making merry and giving gifts to one another" is mentioned, is in Revelation about the two witnesses being killed in the streets of Jerusalem. These men to whom Peter was preaching the resurrection were "stabbed in the heart". They were also Jews and knew the old covenant. And in typical old covenant thinking they asked, "What should we DO?" Peter, still in old covenant thinking, still in tradition, (drawing straws, going to the temple at the hour of prayer) says, "Repent and be baptized." He knew that it was a gift, but thought you had to do something to get it. He thought you had to be baptized in water to receive the gift (and so do some denominations today). They received the gift, not because they were baptized in water but because they had a change of heart, baptized in Spirit. They had godly sorrow, and that leads to repentance. What follows is all they knew to do. They stayed together. They huddled. They went to the Temple, old covenant, but now they also shared everything and clung to each other to keep from being persecuted. This early form of communism failed. Persecution eventually came and the church was on the run. The gospel spread to the rest of the known world. God used this persecution to help the church get out of its cocoon. The plan was Jerusalem...... then all of Judea, then Samaria, then the entire world! However, this model of communism is still used today by some "church" leaders saying that if we do what they did, we will have miracles. The problem is that the goal is miracles, signs and wonders and the method is to use this micro portion of "The book of Acts" as a prescription of "church". This is communism, not church. And it doesn't work. I belonged to a community like this for 15 years; had all things common, breaking of bread house to house, fellowship, read only the Bible, no distractions, no tv, no radio, no electricity, no running water, fastings often, sometimes forty days on water only, teachings of the apostles. It didn't work. Scattering works. Spreading the news works. God used signs, miracles, and wonders to jump start the church, but wouldn't it be difficult to drive down the street with jumper cables still attached to your car? The church was meant to have a generator, to regenerate, multiply, scatter, move, grow, mature, spread like wildfire. And eventually it did. We're not in the jump start phase anymore. We haven't been there for 2000 years. Huddling together is not the model of the gospel. Hearing and running is. Sure we can meet together, but most of our time would be better used being an example in our jobs, in the marketplace and as we travel. It should follow that if we have been saved, born from above, made alive that we would want everyone to know what we've found. We can't help but be good examples and speak of the wonderful things God has done through Jesus. I'm an introvert, but still you can't shut me up, at least planting seeds when I meet new people. It's not about personality, it's about our experience. Was it real. Can you be quiet about it? The church "works" when we preach the gospel AND use words (do and teach), even without miracles. Miracles is not the goal. Witnessing is. Our lives preach the gospel. Anyone can talk. Talking heads can talk. Talk is cheap. Jesus had said, "Is it easier to say, your sins are forgiven or rise and walk?"

Acts 3

THE POINT OF CHAPTER 3 is verse 15. Peter says, yes, there are miracles, but don't focus on the miracle nor the one whom it came through. Focus on Jesus, "whom God raised up from the dead, of which we are witnesses". We are witnesses of the resurrection. Faith comes from resurrection. It is the most important thing God has done. If Christ is not raised from the dead then your faith is vain. It doesn't matter, all the teachings, miracles, signs and wonders, are all pointless without the resurrection. We have been given power......POWER to witness that you may know.....then he healed the paralytic. The proof of resurrection is in a new life. It's our daily walk. It's how I treat my wife, my kids....a stranger..... Relationships are vital to becoming a whole person. Preach the gospel and sometimes use words. The gospel.

Recently, someone said that the gospel was not about the resurrection, but the kingdom because Jesus preached the gospel before he was raised from the dead. Jesus preached the gospel of the kingdom of heaven because he was in the kingdom of heaven. But no one else was and the only way to get into the kingdom of heaven is to be born from above. The only way to be born from above is to be born of Spirit and the only way to be born of Spirit is to receive the Spirit of Jesus which he could not send until he "went away", until he died and ROSE from the dead. So without the resurrection of Jesus, there is no good news of the kingdom. If he hadn't died and rose, we'd STILL be in our sins, and NOT in the kingdom.......not good news (gospel). So when we say the gospel is "Jesus died for our punishment and raised to give us life", that's good news. It's good news for us. Jesus preached the "gospel" of the kingdom that was in him, but was coming to us. He didn't need resurrection. We do. The kingdom was "near", "at hand", in Him but not in us. We couldn't even see it without being born from above (Jn 3: 3). The gospel is the good news that Jesus died for our punishment and rose from the dead to give us new life. Jesus would have been the only man in the kingdom of heaven if he hadn't risen from the dead. Bad news! Matthew 5,6 and 7 would be worthless without the resurrection. Genesis through Malachi would be worthless without the resurrection. Your faith would be vain! (1 Cor 15: 12-19) "But they had the old covenant." Yes, and they were in the place called "Abraham's side" waiting for the Messiah! No one went to "heaven" until Jesus rose from the dead. Jesus was the first raised from the dead to resurrection (Col 1: 18, 1 Cor 15: 20). Enoch and Elijah (Heb 11:13) died and raised after Jesus was raised. Enoch and Elijah visited heaven but had to die and go to Abraham's bosom and wait for the Messiah. Jesus is the first resurrected from the dead. What about Lazarus? He was raised, but not with a glorious, immortal body. He died. He is one of those who will rise first when Jesus comes back. Hebrews 11 says, "these ALL died in faith......NOT having received the promise".

Make no mistake, nothing makes any sense without the resurrection of Jesus, of which I am a witness. We have power to witness. Witness what? A new life. I (speaking of body and mind) am not who I was. I'm a long way (ask my wife) from always being a shining example of Jesus, but I have some moments of new life. I'm changed, not perfect. I'm not sinless, but I sin less. (But my spirit, we are born of the Spirit, who I am, is perfect and sinless, 1 Jn 3:9, that which is born of Spirit doesn't sin). The apostles witnessed about the resurrection. (period). All the rest is accessories. You have to wonder, how this man in verse 2 had not been already healed by Jesus. Jesus passed through here many times. The man was at the temple daily, at the beautiful gate, and had been lame from birth (and what about all those sick people at the pool of Bethesda, why was only one person healed?). Why doesn't Jesus always heal? I don't know for sure, but I think something is missing on our side of the equation. In one place it is stated that Jesus could not heal because of their unbelief. Faith (belief) comes by hearing.....hearing what?.... the Word of God....... red words. The more we think like Jesus, the more we will experience him. However, when he was healed, he "praised God". He didn't question why he wasn't healed before. He didn't praise or worship the apostles. Peter saw an opportunity to preach the resurrection of Jesus. You killed the author of life, but God raised him up from the dead. We are witnesses! Peter goes on to explain to the completely Jewish church who the Jewish Messiah is. Remember the first church is Jewish, a Jewish sect following a Jewish Messiah. As Moses had said, "........one like me; you shall hear him" (Acts 3:22-24). I hope you are looking up these verses, it won't make sense otherwise. The church never ceased to be Jewish. However, wolves came in and changed the rules and instead of Gentiles being included if they became Jewish, the institution called church became Gentile and kicked the Jews out. Sadly, the Jewish Messiah would not be welcome in many institutions called "churches" today, but they don't know that; it would take a renewing of mind to be able to recognize the Christ. Sometimes I wonder if Jesus were to enter some of our more "seeker friendly, worldly friendly, the way the world does it, kind of "churches", would he stand in the back and think, "What in the world are they doing?", "I sang one hymn in all the "gospels" and that was a psalm, and they've turned "worship" into a talent show, an ear damaging talent show, what are they thinking?" "Why are they still preaching the baptism of John?" "Why are they asking people to give their lives to me... and begging for money, threatening them with curses about Tithes? I want to give my life to them". I'm not knocking "The Church". However we should not confuse "The Church" with the thousands of divided institutions that call themselves churches. The Church is a Jewish sect, the Nazarenes, the Way, always has been, always will be. Better to find out what Passover means than to wonder why you didn't get more for xmas. (yeah, xmas is not about the resurrection, but Passover is). Passover is about the Lamb that takes away the sin of the world. If Jesus is not raised from the dead then you are yet in your sins and your faith is vain. "But Christmas is Jesus' birthday, keep Christ in Christ mass".

Really? It's Roman Catholic. Sorry, Catholicism is a denomination too, or rather the mother of all other denominations. If you want to celebrate the winter solstice and have fun and exchange gifts and have family time by all means enjoy; but it's not Christ's birthday; it's not about Jesus. The resurrection is about Jesus. "Oh, you mean like Easter"? No. That's the holiday of fertility with rabbits and eggs and baby chicks. I mean Passover and First Fruits, "as often as you do this (Passover) do it in remembrance of me".

Acts 4

AND WHY WERE THE Sadducees, the Temple commander, and the priests distressed? The resurrection. The Sadducees didn't even believe in resurrection, period, let alone that Jesus was raised from the dead. That's why they were sad, you see. But five thousand believed. Believed what? The resurrection of Jesus. The next day the whole town is in an uproar, the rulers, the elders, the scribes, the high priest, the whole high priestly family. Peter explains, "Jesus Christ, the Nazarene, you killed him; But God raised him from the dead! There is salvation in no other." This is a salvation issue. There is no compromise. Zero tolerance. The gospel is the resurrection for the whole human race and I think that includes everyone. Everyone from Adam, (which does not include Jesus. Jesus is not a descendant of Adam. Jesus had no sin). The rulers didn't know what to do. So what do rulers do when they don't know what to do? They threaten. Verse 17. And what do the believing do when they are threatened? They pray. They ask God to change themselves, to be more bold in speaking his word. And they speak the word of God with boldness. And with great power they give testimony of what? miracles? signs? No. The resurrection of the Lord Jesus. Then great grace comes. This may sound harsh or judgmental, but I'm just making a distinction between the "church" and what we call church. There's nothing wrong with The Church! The real church is working like it should. It's not popular! Constantine made the word "church" and "cross" popular. The cross is a curse. It's a tool of death. It's not jewelry. The church is persecuted. The master was persecuted and he said his followers would be persecuted also. It's not time to reign with him. It's time to suffer with him. Ooh, that's not popular. I'm sorry, it's not your best life now. It's his best now, and that's death, burial and resurrection. The reason people missed Jesus the first time is because they thought he meant he would give them their best life then......restore the kingdom to Israel, squash the Romans, rule and reign. They wanted to hear what they wanted him to mean. And when they saw him go to the cross, they gave up following. The ones that followed, suffered. Read Peter's letters. The reason people miss him now is they are looking for success in the natural, physical world and it is never about the physical. Never. It will all perish, melt, because it is temporary. The kingdom of God is permanent. It is eternal; eternal Life. There is no end. It's not what they thought he meant at first, but they learned. We should learn. Jesus is not Lord over America. Satan is the god of this world. There are no "Christian" countries. Nope, not the Vatican. We live in enemy territory. This is not our home. We are aliens. Or are we?

Years ago, many years ago, in the early 70's Hal Lindsey wrote books about the "last days", predictions, and pretty much the stuff that the fantasy movies about "left behind" and other fanciful interpretations of Revelation are made of today. One of the books was "Satan is alive and well on planet Earth", 1972. Lucifer, meaning "light bearer" was alive once but fell like lightning to earth and has been performing dead works of darkness ever since. His name is not Lucifer anymore, which is not a bad name, but probably no one would name his child that, because of connotation not meaning. Satan is dead, dead to God. There is no salvation for Satan. He will never be alive and certainly he has never done anything well. He is, however here on planet Earth. In old testament times Hal Lindsey would have been stoned as a false prophet because his predictions didn't come to pass. Lesson: Don't predict! The Church, the real Church IS alive and doing well. It has since its inception. And the gates of Hell shall not prevail against it. There are just so many institutions calling themselves "The Church" that we are blinded to the real characteristics of the real Church. Martin Luther and John and Charles Wesley were members of the body of the real Church. But their followers thought they should make a religion out of them. The Church isn't full of hypocrites. Religious institutions called churches are. The real Church is made up of those "born ones" "firstborn ones" (Heb 12:23), trees that bear good fruit, the body of Christ, known by love, disciples, friends of Christ. The Church is not in trouble. The Church is not failing. "Christians" are not falling away from the Church. People may be repulsed by the hypocrisy of the imposters calling themselves "The Church". But the wolf in sheep's clothing isn't fooling the real Church. The Church, the body of Christ, the called out ones, born ones, is alive, vibrant, bearing good fruit, but scattered. There are remnants of the Church in the institutionalized religion called church but they are like double agents, recruiting members of the real Church, not of this world, like treasure hidden in a field. Not fitting into the mold of organized, rituals and superstitions of churchy people is not a sign that you are not a Christian. It could be a sign that you are one. We will never reach the world by being like the world.

When Peter and John returned to "The Church", they prayed (Ac 4:23ff). They prayed for themselves to change. That's the kind of prayer that works. We have no power to change anyone else nor circumstances, but we can change us. They prayed for more boldness to speak..... to speak of what? Only one thing. The most important thing then and now. They gave witness of the resurrection of the Lord Jesus. And great grace was upon them all. They didn't value their possessions over their passion, their commission, their lives. The word for "witness" in the original language, Greek, "martyr" has come to mean something else. The early church, the real church, was willing to die for the gospel. They counted it an honor to be beat for Christ or to die for witnessing about the resurrection. They believed the resurrection. They believed that they would rule and reign with Christ in the future, not now. Not now for them. Not now, for us either. Christianity exploded around the known world. The more they were persecuted and killed the more it spread and Christians were known for dying well. It's quite different today. The trend is prosperity at least here in America. The American gospel is your best life now. Success, beauty, wealth, happiness, beauty, prestige, recognition, beauty, talent, strength, beauty and popularity and did I mention beauty? FACE book. How do I look? It's not just the women. The original word for witness in the book of Acts became synonymous with death and persecution. The word meant to witness or to give testimony but in those days it almost always came with persecution and death. So the word in Greek, "Martyr" came to mean one who dies or suffers for what he believes and means such in our vocabulary in English today. It was normal then to speak with boldness and be thrown to the lions, or burned at the stake, or be beheaded for your "witness".

It's different today. Another religion is growing now. Islam is adding numbers like wildfire. The religion promises rewards after you die. If you die for the cause you get seventy virgins in heaven. I don't know what women get. They don't seem to value women at all. We, the United States, threaten to kill Muslim terrorists when they kill our own. That's just what they want. That's what motivates them: to be killed promoting their religion. So we are lulled to sleep spiritually by a false sense of security "God loves the USA" and they are multiplying like rabbits. America is not a Christian nation. The only Christian nation is "The Church". The real one. And the benefits of this Christian nation are spiritual, not carnal; it's never about the physical. "The Church" is not losing. The Church is winning.......the lost. It's hidden. It's behind the scenes. It's not in the spotlight. The "Church" is all about the resurrection of Jesus and the spirit life he gives us. Are you saying we can't have any fun? What I'm saying is that the life of Jesus, the words of Jesus, the thoughts of Jesus are the most important things to real Christians. You can look at a person's life and tell what they value. Isn't that judgmental? A spiritual man judges all things. Things not people. I can look at my own life and see what I value. To die is gain. To live is for others' benefit. "Easy for you to say, Glenn, you're old and almost dead anyway. I'm young and have my whole life ahead of me!" I want to _____ (fill in the blank), before I die. I'm just sayin', we don't have the same mindset as the early "Church".

The idea isn't to guilt us into "doing" what the early church did. That's a prescription. The account of what the Apostles thought and did is a description not a prescription. If we want a prescription, it would have to begin with our mindset; what we value. We would have to change our thinking, then we would behave differently. That would be a lifestyle not a religion or ritual to be performed once or twice a year, or once or twice a week, or once or twice a day. It's just not about performance, (everyone give the Lord a clap offering; on second thought, I don't think he wants one). It's really not the book of "Acts". It's the book of "fruit" of the True Vine. It's what happens when disciples follow and love one another as Jesus loved us. It's the book of Love. And you can't prescribe how love will manifest. We love and do. We receive and give. And it's better to give than to receive. We love because he first loved (and died for) us. It's the book of what happens when we believe in the resurrection of the Lord Jesus.

He's alive! He is risen! How does that impact your life and consequently the lives of others. "Yeah, you're right, but nobody's perfect and right now I'm just hungry, where do you wanna go for lunch?" Pray! now. We all have our dull moments. Pray. Ask Jesus to speak to you as you read his words, (red words) and give you convictions. Not convict you. Convicts go to jail. You are free. But have convictions, things that you believe that are spiritually life giving. He won't change you, but you will change if you listen to him and let his sayings sink down deep into your spiritual ears.

Joses was such a person, called Barnabas, (Bar-Nabas, or Son-of-Consolation) by the Apostles. He was a giver. But Ananias was not; he was a poser and not a very good one. This is what happens when you try to mimic or imitate fruit (prescription) instead of being and bearing fruit.

Acts 5

S OMETIMES THESE CHAPTER BREAKS are just plain disruptive. Remember in the original there were no chapter and verse breaks. What did Ananias and his wife do that was so wrong? They died because of it? Whoa, still want to be part of "The Church"? Don't worry, they weren't Christians. They were not the "church". They were imposters. Satan filled their hearts, not Jesus. Sin is not the doing of a deed but the violation of a principle. They were children of the Devil. The fruit in their lives was tell-tale. "And you shall know them by their fruits", Jesus had said. (Mt 7:20) Peter knew this. The violation of the principle was that they tempted the Spirit of the Lord. Bad idea. Satan tempts the Spirit of the Lord; that's what he does. The Lord is not tempted, but Satan tempts, that's who he is. "Okay.......... what? The Lord is not tempted but Satan tempts?" Yes, James explains in James 1:13ff. In Hebrews 3:8 the Israelites tempted God! Was God tempted? No. So there's tempting going on from the tempter on the outside but not on the inside of the one who is the object of this temptation. Suppose you never smoked a cigarette and had no desire to, and you're with a friend who is trying to quit. Someone walks up and offers a smoke. This is temptation. But not for you, only for the one who is trying to quit. That person is tempted within himself. There's nothing in you that wants that cigarette so no matter how often or how insistent the tempter is, there is no temptation for you. But yet there is tempting going on. You are being tempted. But only because the other person is tempting you, not because there is anything in you that is tempted. (This is what happened to Jesus on the pinnacle of the temple. You didn't think he really wanted to jump did you?). Jesus could not sin. Jesus was not capable of sinning. Jesus was not able to do anything that he didn't see his Father doing, spiritually (Jn 5:19).

Great fear came on everyone, the church and the onlookers. The onlookers responded with, "I wouldn't dare be part of that!" and the "believing" responded by being added to the church and bringing their loved ones to be healed. Ananias and Sapphira weren't killed for not giving enough money. They weren't killed for lying. They weren't killed at all. They were already spiritually dead, children of Satan, and Satan had filled their hearts. Their physical bodies succumbed under the weight of their sinful nature and sinful choices. This was a consequence of their life choices. There is a spirit world; we would do well to pay attention; whatever we plant is what we grow. Apple seeds grow apple trees. If we plant fleshly sinful desires, we grow fleshly sinful lives. Be careful what you plant. It's just not a good idea to bounce through life like a pin ball randomly going downhill until we exit. It's not much better to try to change our behavior. When we receive Christ, our spirit is born, we become new because of what he's done. Then we can change our minds (soul) to think like him and grow. It's not "Think and Grow Rich", it's "Think and Grow", (bear fruit of the Spirit - Love, real love, sacrificial love).

So, someone was wondering, "Why does God kill people"? I think that's a valid question and I'm not sure there is a complete answer for us finite thinkers. God's ways are above our ways and I agree with Paul, ".......His ways are past finding out......." (Rom 11:33). However, we can know some things and we can know God's character. In the beginning God created man and had a wonderful relationship with him and man was to live forever. What changed? God didn't "kill" man but warned that if he ate of the" tree of the knowledge of good and evil" (whatever that was; it wasn't an apple tree), he would surely die that same day. They ate but didn't "die" physically. They died spiritually and needed a savior. But now their bodies were "dying" and eventually died. There are consequences of our actions in the physical world for our disobedience in the spirit world. In the Old Covenant one man tried to "save" the Ark of the Covenant from falling and God was angry and struck him dead (1 Ch 13:9). So what was going on? We have limited understanding. The Chronicles were written by Godly men but they weren't perfect and wrote in their own understanding. The finger of God did not write the Chronicles like He wrote the ten commandments. God did not move their hands and fingers to write. So, Uzzah did die. He died because God had said, "Don't touch the Ark of the Covenant or you will die" (Num 4:15). Uzzah's intentions were to "save" the Ark from falling but the command was in place and the consequences of violating that command were also. We will all die physically some day, unless Jesus comes back first. In the old covenant people could be in covenant with God and obey and when they died go to a place of waiting, Abraham's bosom, until Jesus was resurrected, then be resurrected with him. In the new covenant, Jesus paid for our punishment and when we die physically we will be with him if we have been born from above. Our spiritual life or death is up to us. That's the simplicity of it. But we are more curious and complicated than that and more concerned about the timing of our physical death and the death of our loved ones. We always ask "why?", when someone close dies. That's the part we don't know. The "when" and "why" people die physically is unknown. What we do know is that physical death is a consequence of Adam's sin. We all die physically. Some die as a direct result of their actions and some don't. That's a "why" and we don't know. Did God kill Uzzah? Did God kill Ananias and Sapphira? Did God kill Judas Iscariot? Did God kill my child? No. Death is the consequence of Adam's sin. The timing of our death is not knowable and children that don't reach an age to be able to make a mature choice go back to God. That' s what I believe.

Many miracles and wonders took place among the people through the hands of the apostles. They were persecuted, put in jail and the "church" grew. Peter thought it was only for Israel, "to give to Israel repentance and forgiveness". This is still old covenant thinking, "You have to repent to be forgiven, and it's only for Israel". Peter was so sure he said that the "Holy Spirit" was witness to these things as well, that God only gave to those who obey. That's old covenant. That's not a prescription. That's earned and limited to Jews. That's not the Holy Spirit, that's Peter. It's awkward to point this out. Miracles were happening through the man that's saying things that don't seem to line up with what God will be doing. The Holy Spirit, God in Christ will be offering salvation to Gentiles soon and all they have to do is confess and believe. How could Peter be getting it wrong when there are miracles being done through him? Because miracles are never the test of correct teaching. Peter wasn't wrong, just not informed. He connected the dots he had until God showed more. But when God shows more we should change our thinking. Smith Wigglesworth and Kathryn Kuhlman didn't have all the answers. They had miracles.

And like the rest of us, limited understanding. What was the fruit of this exhibit of miracles and preaching of Peter? They wanted to kill him. The church wasn't growing because of miracles and limited understanding. The "church" was growing because people were hungry and touched by God. We plant, we water, but only God grows people. Gamaliel spoke: If this is from God, you can't stop it. I agree. Churches that fail are not "the Church". And by failing, we don't mean numbers. We mean no fruit, no love, no relationships. They are plans of men, and plans of men fail. Love never fails!

The "Church" is alive and well. The real church is growing, is loving, is forgiving, is accepting. That being said, when someone encounters the real church, they change. An encounter with the real church is an encounter with Jesus, the Spirit of Jesus, the Holy Spirit, God. And the fruit is change. The hand that stole, steals no more; the tongue that lied, tells the truth; and sexual immorality is a thing of the past. If that doesn't happen, something didn't work. A good tree bears good fruit. One who is born of Spirit bears spiritual fruit. In the Spirit, born from above, a new creature in the spirit, we don't sin. In the spirit realm we are born to be alive to God and dead to sin. Our minds and body are not born of spirit and so there is a residue of sin in the mind. We must pursue the renewing of the mind that transforms the body. (Rom 12:1-2) How does this look? Sinners become saints. I was a sinner, and all I could do was sin; a slave to sin; dead to God and alive to sin. But when the law came, sin revived and I died. I was born from above.

The real me, the spirit being that was dead to God was born of God. I am a child of God (in the spirit), I don't sin (in the spirit), I am a saint (in the spirit). I sometimes sin (in the mind and body) but less. My mind is changing and my body follows. I am saved. I have eternal life (in the spirit). But the mind must follow or with our minds we could reject salvation. Not that doing a deed could take away eternal life but we could get to a place where like Esau said, "What good is my birthright, I'm starving ?" and not have our salvation taken away, but we could reject it. My life is not the same, not sinless but I sin less. And less and less. That's growth and a new life should grow. We don't need to judge each other; we can judge ourselves.

We are not judging Peter. Peter worked with the knowledge he had until more was revealed......even in a trance! Even Peter's shadow healed people!!!...... well, God healed, he used Peter. The Sad-you-see's (who didn't believe in resurrection) tried to lock them up, but angels let them out. This happened then but later on Paul would be confined to prison and house arrest. The apostles would be beaten and killed, Peter would be hung upside down on a cross, but not now. Things happened but this isn't a plan book. It's just a description. The only thing we are guaranteed is the Holy Spirit will live in us. That is our reward. That is ETERNAL life. Now and later. Were we looking for something to add to that shopping cart? Maybe streets of gold, precious stones, mansions over the hilltop? Crowns? You can't add anything to eternal life...... nothing else is eternal! "Oh, well, what are we gonna do... sit on clouds and play harps all day?" I've literally heard this. But no, clouds and harps are not eternal. We are spirit beings that have inherited spirit life. Well, what does that mean? "Eye has not seen, nor ear heard, nor has it risen in the heart of man, the things God has prepared for those who love him". But God has revealed them to us! by his SPIRIT! (1 Cor 2: 9-16). We have access to the mind of Christ and we can renew our minds to his, BY HIS SPIRIT! There are billions of galaxies each containing billions of solar systems that one day could be populated; of his kingdom there is no end..................that could keep us busy for a while!

Again, when released, they preached the resurrection: "The God of our fathers raised up Jesus, whom you laid hands on, hanging him on a tree. We are his witnesses! God didn't die on the cross, the man Christ Jesus did and God raised him up. We are witnesses! Not just Jehovah's Witnesses but Jehovah Saves witnesses. Jesus is the English form through Latin and Greek back to Hebrew of Yahshua or Yahweh Shua or Jehovah Saves. We are in the NEW testament! Well, some of us are.

Those hearing wanted to kill them. But Gamaliel spoke and they obeyed him. But they still beat the apostles and commanded them not to teach the resurrection. But everyday they did not cease to preach the gospel of Jesus the Christ......The resurrection!

Acts 6

COMMUNITIES, COMMUNES, PEOPLE LIVING together having "all things common", kibbutz' will always have conflict. Wherever two or three are gathered there will be politics, and jealousy and etc. This was no different and the Greek speaking Jewish believers, Hellenists, were offended because their widows weren't being given care. So they appointed disciples to do just that. Stephen was one. Full of faith he did miracles among them. But of course others were jealous and stirred up false witnesses to say that Stephen was speaking against Moses and God, against this place and the law. Well, that's what insecure people do. When questioned before the "high priest", a Sadducee, (doesn't believe in resurrection), Stephen reminds them of their history. And we should know this history. I can't explain it any better than Stephen and won't try. But please read all of Acts 7.

Acts 7

W E PICK IT UP in verse 48, "The most high doesn't live in temples made with man's hands". Then Stephen called out their resistance to the Holy Spirit because they betrayed and murdered the "Just One". They were cut to the heart and they dragged him out to be stoned to death, meanwhile Stephen is "seeing the glory of God, The son of man standing at the right hand" (please think spiritual) of God. Remember, God is not a man and doesn't have human hands. Jesus Christ, however, is a man and died and was RESURRECTED! That's the point. Stephen was witnessing about the resurrection. Then Stephen forgave them. Enter Saul. (who later becomes Paul). Saul/ Paul witnessed all of this. He heard Stephen speak. He heard Stephen forgive. God was preparing his vessel for ministry at the expense of Stephen. God knows what he's doing, whether we can figure it out or not.

Acts 8

G OD'S FIRST ATTEMPT AT Saul (Stephen's witness) didn't seem to take. He kept on persecuting the "Church". Don't give up on lost ones, God doesn't. The scattering was on and the gospel (the resurrection), the "word" was being preached by Philip with miracles. The local magician liked what he saw and thought he could add this to his act. No one was baptized in spirit yet only in water and consequently no one was born from above or born of spirit yet. They were dunked in water saying "in the name of Jesus" but they had not received the Spirit. But then they did when the apostles laid their hands on them. The magician thought it was some kind of ritual or magical transference because they laid their hands on them, like an initiation rite or something, so he offered to pay his way with money for this ability that Philip had. Wrong focus. It's not about miracles and magic. It's a gift of God. It's spiritual. It's about the resurrection of Jesus. Peter said, You ain't right. Repent. Maybe God will forgive you. Simon, the magician, said, Pray for me. We don't know how that turned out. I think Simon came around and got saved.

An angel appears to Philip and tells him to go to the Gaza strip on the way to Africa. He meets up with an Ethiopian eunuch from the Queen Candice's palace on his way back from Jerusalem, (probably a Jew returning from Pentecost/ Shavuot) reading from Isaiah. Through some dialogue the Ethiopian asks Philip to explain these verses and Philip tells him about the resurrection, "preached to him the gospel of Jesus". The eunuch believed Jesus to be the son of God and was baptized in Spirit, born of Spirit, born from above, saved. But then he wanted to be baptized in water. This was traditional even in Ethiopia, but obviously not required to believe! He believed first. He wanted to be baptized in water because he believed. When the eunuch comes up out of the water, Philip's gone. No classes, no "discipleship", no programs, no membership classes......well, you get the point. The eunuch's relationship was based on God's word from Isaiah and then on Jesus' words through Philip. Of course we will gravitate to people of like mind and will tell others about Jesus, but that's fruit not rules, regulations, requirements and commanded obedience. "But........Jesus said, "Going then, disciple all nations, baptizing them in the name of the Father, and of the son, and of the Holy Spirit; teaching them to observe all things, whatever I commanded you". Wonder what he meant? They heard what they thought he meant. We hear what we think he means. That's not what Philip did. Unless. Well, unless it doesn't mean what we think it does. What if Jesus was saying that baptism is in spirit, the spirit of Father, Son, Holy Spirit? That his name is the name above all names, Jesus? That Yahweh Shua or Yeshua is the name of the Father, Son and Spirit because God is a spirit, one. What if all the commandments were now contained in the last commandment, the new commandment that Jesus gave? "Love one another as I have loved you, Love one another!" (Jn 13:34) "By THIS all men shall know you are my disciples! If you have love one to another!" Maybe? Fruit. Fruit of the Spirit, the Spirit of Father in Christ, love. Hmmmmmm. Do we hear what he meant? Philip went on witnessing about the resurrection, preaching "the gospel".

Acts 9

S AUL, STILL ZEALOUS FOR "the Lord" without a clue, murdering the disciples, asks the high priest of non believers in the resurrection for permission to pursue the synagogues of Damascus. He's looking for "the church", which in those days was called "the way", just one, one church, one way, believers in the resurrection of Jesus, that's all. Maybe we should follow that as prescription..... No denominations. No rules, just right. No CEO's called pastors. no buildings called churches........ just meeting in houses. Maybe.

Now we suppose Saul/Paul was on a horse, and a bright light caused him to fall to the earth, and he heard, "Saul, Saul, why do you persecute me?" Saul was like, "Who are you, Lord?" And the Lord said, "I am Jesus, whom you persecute." Saul was murdering followers of Jesus, the Way, believers of the resurrection of Jesus, but Jesus says that Saul was persecuting Jesus. Sometimes we fail to realize the depth of relationship Jesus has with us, his children, his body; he says he is us; we are him; we are one. The world doesn't get this. Satan has no idea what this means. But we, the body of Christ ought to live by it. We are one. There is one body. There are no divisions in the body of Christ. Denominations are hindrances to the body. The only reason we have different beliefs is that we don't know "The only True God and Jesus Christ whom he has sent" enough. (Jn 17, the key to unity).

Apparently, Saul/Paul remembered more of the story when he recounted it to King Agrippa in the 26th chapter. Or Luke remembered more or Luke got the whole story later on. We forget that this is just information written down by men about the history of the "church". I know some want to call it "scripture" but like we've discovered before (*A View Worth Teaching* by this same author under the pen name Tim Tyler), "scripture" only applies to old testament writings, the Tanakh. This can be such a sore subject for those who want to repeat what they've heard with no real biblical (or scriptural) evidence. Not only do we hear what we think Jesus said, we also repeat what others think Jesus said without questioning. The evidence is that every time the word "scripture" is used in the collection of books, letters and gospels we call the Bible it always refers to the writings of the TaNaKh or the "Old Testament" or The Hebrew Bible. Now that's offensive to some even though it's true and factual, Biblical and "Scriptural"! On top of that some want to say that all of the Bible is the Word of God. Well, certainly the Bible contains the Word of God, but firstly, Jesus Christ is the Word of God. Consequently, everything that proceeds from his mouth is the Word of God. And Hebrews 1:1-2 tells us that God, in times past, spoke (Word of God) through the prophets. So the words of the prophets WERE the Word of God and scripture. The Words of Jesus ARE the Word of God but not scripture, by Bible definition; they are the gospel. Now here's the hard part, everything else in the T-orah, N-eviim, K-etuvim or TNK or TaNaK or what we call the "Old Testament", is scripture, simply meaning "the writings" (Graphe in Greek 1124 in Strong's Greek dictionary meaning writing), but not all were the words of God. We have writings (scripture) that Job's friends said, which are scripture but certainly not God's words. We have words spoken to God by Satan, words spoken to Eve by Satan and words by so many ungodly people, false prophets, kings, enemies of God that are not the words of God. So it is all true, they did say those things and the Bible records it accurately, truth; however, not everything everyone said are the Words of God. We have confused the meaning of the word "scripture" (writings) with "The Word of God". In the Gospels and Epistles which we call the New Testament we find the Words of God but biblically speaking by biblical definition they are not scripture. There is not one verse that refers to "New Testament books" as "scripture". I know there is one verse out of context that talks about Paul's writings in 2 Pet 3:16, but the original language, Greek, actually says "the remaining scriptures" referring to the scrolls of the Tanakh that remain. This is mistranslated to say the "other" scriptures meant to imply that Paul's writings are scripture like the "others". Again, one verse, out of context, mistranslated to "prove" a whole doctrine. I believe God gave us the whole Bible. Some believe that the Apocrypha should be included because it was in the Greek version of the "Old Testament" that Jesus quoted from, the Septuagint. Either way, I use and quote the whole Bible but only refer to Jesus words as the Word of God because he is the Word of God who lived in flesh, not became flesh. (Another point of confusion: The word in Jn 1:14 is "egeneto" in original Greek language, 1079 in Strong's dictionary, meaning "birth", but the translator puts the number 1096, which is "ginomai" and means" to become", and translates that the WORD "became" flesh. The WORD, the Spirit, can never become flesh. Yet this is the one verse, mistranslated, out of context, in English, that is used to "prove" that God "became" a man. God is not a man that he should lie nor the son of man that he should repent (Num 23:19, 1 Sam 15:29) and will never "become" a man; He is Spirit and spirit never becomes flesh. He did "birth" his son of a woman and dwelled with us "in" a fleshly tabernacle, just like it says 4637 in Strong's "and tabernacled with us", still in the same verse). The words of the prophets were the Word of God in the old covenant but now God speaks through his Son only (Heb 1:1-2). I believe the whole Bible is correct and true but it is not all called "Scripture", even by those who wrote it.

Saul was led by his men to Damascus where he ended up in the house of Judas, blind and not eating for three days. Ananias meets him, he is filled with the power of the Holy Spirit and witnesses to the resurrection of Jesus, proving that Jesus of Nazareth is the Messiah (Christ) to the Jews in the synagogues. They tried to kill him. He escapes to Jerusalem to be with the disciples but they were afraid of him so Barnabas embraces him and takes him to the Apostles and they heard his story. The Hellenists get offended and try to kill him so he is sent back to Tarsus where he came from. Everyone was happy.

So we have different accounts of the same story in different chapters (9,22,26). Saul had a miraculous encounter with the Lord, he was filled with the power of the Holy Spirit, and he witnessed in the synagogues. But then it was over. We want our witness to just keep growing and reach more and more people but sometimes, no matter how great an experience we have, God is not finished preparing us and it takes some more years. In Moses' case 40, John the Baptist, 30, Jesus, 30. Years! We get in a hurry. But the only person that was told to "do what you must do quickly" was Judas Iscariot. We are important to God, more than we realize, Jesus saying that to persecute us is to persecute him, but at times we think we're more important than other believers and we should be speaking and they should be listening. Saul/Paul was gone for three years (Gal 1:15ff).

Some have wondered why the different gospels by different authors say different things about the life of Jesus and his sayings. It's just natural for us to repeat things differently and remember things differently as we recount them. This is one author, Luke, and he has three different versions of the same story. This doesn't cause a problem if we understand that men merely recorded what they remembered. If, however, we think that Almighty God caused the hands of these men to move and write the "Word of God" supernaturally, well, then there's going to be a problem. God doesn't change. But the writings do. It is enough to believe that Jesus Christ is God in the flesh. It is enough to take his words as the Word of God. His words are Spirit and Life and are enough to "save" us. We should be able to read the words of the apostles as instruction of how to apply Jesus' words to our culture and time and daily lives by telling us how they applied Jesus' teachings to their lives. The lives of the apostles however are not a template for us to follow verbatim. It reminds me of wood staining. If you stain white pine with cherry stain, it turns very red. But if you use the exact same stain on oak, it gives it a slightly reddish tint. The principles that Jesus lived and taught are the same, but the application may be different in our society. The healings that Jesus performed were always different and unpredictable in application: one time, spitting on clay, another speaking from a different town, another laying his hands on. However, his intention, his motive, his character and principle was always the same....... compassion.

So whether the other men heard a voice and saw no one, or saw the light and heard no voice or Paul fell to the ground, or they all fell to the ground doesn't validate the story nor invalidate the story. Luke is giving us early church history; that's all. I don't believe Luke's hand nor any of the other authors of the epistles hands were being moved by God, like a Ouija board. I have found that most denominations don't believe that either, however, the people who just go to church and don't really read or study, do. The church was never meant to be magical, or even supernatural, just spiritual which sometimes results in supernatural phenomena. I say this because so many of the people who attend church, that I have spoken to as a pastor and counselor have been disappointed because their "prayers" weren't answered. God never promised us gratification of the flesh. He promised us a new life in the Spirit. Paul, himself, prayed three times for the thorn in his flesh to be taken away and God said, "No, my grace is enough for you" (2 Cor 12: 8-9). We are saved by grace and it is enough. Our new life in the Spirit and that abundantly (in the Spirit) is enough. Or is it?

Saul/Paul was blind for three days and didn't eat or drink. Ananias put his hands on Paul and told him, "that he may see again (Part1) and be filled with the Holy Spirit (Part 2)". Then the scales fell from his eyes and he saw again, (Part 1) and he was baptized (Part 2), he was filled with the Holy Spirit, not dunked in water. He was baptized in Spirit, which is what Jesus came to do. Saul/Paul began to witness about Jesus being the Messiah, the Jewish Messiah (the Christ, in Greek) in the Jewish synagogues. The Jews sought to kill him. The believers were afraid of him not believing that he was a disciple. Ananias heard the Lord speak to him in a vision. Ananias heard the Lord! But still wanted to inform the Lord that Saul was not one of the good guys and was he sure that he wanted him to go to this Saul. What would I do? What would you do? But Barnabas reached out to him. We all need a Barnabas sometime and we should all be a Barnabas sometime. The apostles sent him home, back to Tarsus. Everyone was relieved.

Sometimes even if one is telling God's truth, the believers feel better if the outspoken ones are not around stirring things up.

Then a miracle. Many miracles took place through the apostles. Many miracles could still be happening today if we believed. What? What do you mean? Why aren't you doing miracles? Don't you believe? What gives you the right? Those questions won't help. The apostles believed and miracles happened. I believe the same power is available today. We just don't think the way they did about miracles. For them it was the result of believing. Today, we seem to need that phenomenon to believe. I don't think that the signs, miracles and wonders ceased with the apostles. I believe however, that we have lost the belief and thinking that precedes this kind of move of the Spirit. We lack something. God still heals. There are still miracles. I have witnessed it in my own family. We had xrays and God miraculously healed. We just don't seem to have the spiritual awareness that is able to call it, to speak it into existence. It seems random. And the typical answer to "Why doesn't God heal more often?" is "We don't know". Well, I think I do know, now. We lack either knowledge or relationship. We are missing something. God is the same. We must allow our thinking to change. "So Glenn, are you saying that you're closer now to being able to "heal" people?" No. That's not the goal. If I can think like Jesus, then I can behave like Jesus. Trouble is, I've got decades of "stinkin' thinkin'" to overcome. Jesus chose young people, quite possibly teenagers to be his disciples. One of the reasons I think he did this was because older people tend to say, "The old way is better" being like cement, all mixed up and permanently set. Instead of "indoctrinating" our young people with "religious" thinking that has given us what we've got, I think we should encourage them to read the red words and think as the Spirit leads, letting the Bible interpret itself. Moody Bible Institute is one of the biggest seminaries in the country. But, Dwight L. Moody for whom it was named, didn't go to a Bible school. He read his Bible. We should stop telling young people "what to think" and just tell them "to think".........about Jesus' words. But then they might turn the world upside down and show us "spiritual, intellectual, holy, experienced" older people up.

Peter raises the dead! But there was more important work to do. What could be more important than raising the dead? I know what that kind of publicity that would cause today! But they weren't seeking publicity. God was initiating a movement. The "church" was going to reach the Gentiles and include them. The Jewish sect of the Nazarenes, the Jewish movement called the Way was going to let Gentiles in! Of course, God has always included the Gentiles making a way for them to enter the camp of the children of Israel as "strangers in the camp". God told Abraham that he would be the father of many "nations" (ethnos, Gentiles, same word 1484 Strong's Greek and 1471 Goy in Hebrew) or the father of many Gentiles. Sounds odd doesn't it? God has always included everyone.

Acts 10

ENTER CORNEILIUS. AN ITALIAN. Not a Jew, but recognized as one who fears God and a just man according to all the nation of the Jews (10:22). Again, let me encourage you to read all of chapter 10 of Acts first, then we can discuss what we've read and compare it to other Bible verses to let the Bible interpret itself. This chapter is loaded with information that has been misquoted, misapplied and misapprehended. In other words there's a lot of preconceived ideas from wrong interpretation of this chapter that have been used to "prove" popular but false doctrines. Let's take it slowly, in the context of the whole Bible, and verse by verse we can arrive at some natural, logical conclusions.

Having said that I do realize that it is hard to change our thinking about things we grew up with or have learned and taken as "gospel" for years. Recently, well, in the last three years, I've found it hard to keep from gaining weight. Certain physical limitations make it hard to exercise like I used to. For the past twenty years or so, I followed the conventional wisdom........a low fat diet. But it wasn't working. I learned about the effects of sugar and carbohydrates that turn to sugar, namely, that unused sugar is stored as fat. Unused fat is eliminated and not stored. So, I cut the carbs.....way down. No breads, pastas, obvious sugars, sweets, fruits. I lost thirty five pounds in three months! It worked. Now, after three years I've added a little here and there but kept twenty five pounds off. A family member knows what I did and watched closely and has seen the lasting results but to this day can't shake the idea that fat causes fat. The facts are there. The logic is there. The experience is there. Proof. But we've talked and she admits the only thing keeping her from accepting it is her old thinking. It's hard to change our thinking. But, if we want to bad enough we can. So we grow up hearing different things about what Jesus said. We have mindsets about certain passages.

In our book, *The Samaritan Woman You Never knew,* we looked at four different women in the New Testament that got a bad rap because of false preconceptions. It happens. This chapter has been used to "prove" that when Jesus died on the cross and rose from the dead pigs were cleansed! I have spoken with people who have a hard time accepting that there is no more judgment for the born from above believer (Jn 5:24), that we are cleansed, cleansed from all sin, past, present and future and there is now no condemnation (Rom 8:1) but swallow the idea that it's good to eat pork because God cleansed it in Christ. They find it easier to believe that pigs got cleansed at the cross than people. Again, I would like to read this chapter in Acts without preconceived ideas.

At three in the afternoon an angel appears to Cornelius and says that God has heard his prayers. He had been fasting from the fourth day (four days?)(verse 30) and a man in bright clothing appears and tells him to send *three* men to Peter in the city of Joppa and Peter will tell him what to do. As these *three* men approach the city, Peter is on the roof to pray at noon (Peter is still keeping ritual; not a bad ritual, but not required). Peter got hungry. Well, it was noon and sure, that's just one of the distractions to praying isn't it? So while lunch is being fixed, Peter falls into a trance or vision and "sees" something that resembles a huge net with all kinds of animals and beasts and birds and "creeping things" being lowered from heaven. A voice says, "Get up and kill and eat". Peter says, "No way! I've never eaten anything unclean". Remember Peter is Jewish; he's an Israelite from Galilee of the Gentiles. The voice says, "What God has cleansed, do not make common or unclean". This happened *three* times. Then it was over. Peter was at a total loss, mentally. What could that possibly mean? Go kill a pig and eat it three times?

Rattlesnake, mice, crayfish? But while he was perplexed the *three* men show up. The Spirit said, "I sent *three* men to you, don't judge"! Peter let them spend the night and probably fed them. Then the next day they all go to see Cornelius. There were a bunch of Gentiles there. Peter says, "You know it's unlawful for me being a Jew to come near to one of another race". But God showed me. Okay, it was Peter's vision, for Peter, so Peter gets to interpret the vision for us. He says, "But God showed me not to call a MAN common or unclean" (verse 28) (three times, three men). Peter might have been thinking, "okay, so we went through all this vision and perplexity and interpretation, so now what?" so he asks, "I came, so why did you send for me"? Cornelius tells his story and Peter responds with, "I perceive that God is no respecter of persons, but is willing to accept everyone". Now that's a great perception! "Jesus of Nazareth, God anointed him with the Holy Spirit and power. He healed because God was with him. We are witnesses! God raised him up! To be visible to witnesses. (witnesses of the resurrection) He commanded us to witness about the resurrection. All the prophets witnessed about him and everyone believing him receives remission of sins."

As Peter was still speaking, the Holy Spirit came to those hearing the word. The Jews were amazed that this happened to Gentiles! They heard them speaking in languages, magnifying God. Sounds like chapter 2: 4-6. They heard them magnifying God, speaking in languages or tongues. So they knew what they were saying if they heard them magnifying God. Remember, Luke always refers to known languages or the physical tongue when using the Greek word "glossa". Glossolalia or the speaking of random syllables of unknown language, or "gibberish" has been a phenomenon for thousands of years in many religions including Voodoo and Hindu and as modern as Mormon. It simply means that the speaker expresses verbally, random utterances that are not any known language and helps the speaker express things that he doesn't know how to express in a known language. This can be very helpful psychologically for someone who needs that kind of expression. Although this has been thought to be "spiritual" and

"Christian" and even "super Christian", there is no real basis for that in the Bible nor the early church. Google it. I wouldn't condemn it but I wouldn't encourage it publicly and here I agree with Paul in his letter to the Corinthian church. He addresses the phenomena of glossolalia. He says the one speaking in a "tongue" does not speak to men but to God; for no one hears, but in spirit he speaks mysteriously. But the one prophesying (speaking) to men speaks for building up, encouragement and comfort (1 Cor 14:1ff). He goes on to say in verse 9 that "you will be speaking into the air" and that in verse 19, "I'd rather speak five intelligent words than myriads (thousands) in glossolalia or a "tongue". He says, "Grow up!" "Be mature in your minds! If someone does speak in public with this practice, then someone interpret or say something that will encourage the church. Remember, we want the unbeliever to come to our gatherings and hear about salvation through Jesus. If they come to our meetings and someone is babbling in unknown gibberish, speaking into the air, he'll think we're insane! "(Paraphrase). I wouldn't forbid it, but do it at home, when you talk to God and if you think you know what it means then if it is encouraging for the church, bring it, decently and in order. That's what Paul wrote later to the church at Corinth and that's all he says about it. There is no indication anywhere in the Bible nor in early church history that glossolalia is any "sign" that someone is more "spiritual" than anyone else. "Yes, but, Glenn, Jesus said, in Mark 16, that, 'they will speak in new languages'. Red words, Glenn"! I know. Next, it says, "they will take up snakes". Anybody up for that? And we've seen the three ring circus that's turned into. Mark 16: 9-20 does not appear in the two oldest manuscripts and its authenticity is disputed. I wouldn't use these verses as the foundation of a doctrine; they might not be red words.

Then Peter, in his traditional, ritual, thinking says, "Now that they've received the baptism of the Spirit, why not baptize them in water too"? (John's baptism? Why? Acts 11: 16-17, the Word of the Lord! "but" you will be baptized in the Holy Spirit"). The only point being made about water baptism is that it is not required. It's a great way for someone to identify with a certain fellowship of believers. It's a great way to give someone the opportunity to profess their faith. Water baptism is a good tradition of the "church". I've been baptized four times. My wife and daughter were baptized in the Jordan River. But, it's just tradition. It's not required for salvation. It's not required for growth. I recommend it for a feeling of a new beginning. It's something to be celebrated. However, to say any physical act or work is required for salvation or growth is just not spiritual. Everything Jesus said was spiritual. If we make it physical, we'll miss the point. "But", there's always a "but", "Glenn, Jesus said,

'Going then, disciple all nations, baptizing them into the name of the Father, Son and Holy Spirit; teaching them to observe all things whatever I commanded you' (Mt 28:19). What do you do with that verse" ? Well, again, we don't build doctrines with one verse. Jesus' parting words should be a repeat of what he had already done and taught them before. We found out that a disciple is one who learns the TaNaKh (Jews), believes in Jesus and continues in HIS word. Then, they can know The Truth (Jesus) and The Truth (Jesus) will make them free, according to Jn 8:31-32. We also found that the "nations" or the world, ALL, will know that we are his disciples if we have love one to another (Jn 13:34). This is the "new" commandment. The new commandment supersedes and includes all previous commands. Love fulfills the Law and the prophets and fulfills love God and love your neighbor. 1 Corinthians 13 type love fulfills the new commandment. Could it be that Jesus was speaking spiritually and saying in his last instructions to his disciples, "As you go, show all men, nations, "ethnos", that you are my disciples, by having love one to another, thereby giving them an example to follow, thereby making "disciples" who love one another; thereby immersing them into the character of the Father and of the Son and of the Holy spirit; teaching them (by example) to observe all things that I commanded YOU (to observe YOU keeping the new commandment that I gave to you). Otherwise, we interpret it to mean something that we do to them not what we do and they follow. Hundreds of years later the Crusaders got it all wrong and "thought" they were serving God, obeying Jesus and led by the Holy Spirit to force Muslims to be baptized in water or get their heads cut off, according to the "scriptures" in Jesus Name! We are still, to this day, suffering retaliation from radical Muslims for that. The gospel is "good" news and makes people free. It is never about rules and regulations and requirements to be in the club. Could "make disciples" mean love one another? All churches? All denominations? Could it mean be an example of love? Could Jesus be speaking about the baptism HE came to give? Baptizing in the Spirit; immersing in the Spirit of Father and Son. Could he have meant that "doing" this would "teach" them to see or observe what Jesus commanded us? Namely, to love one another? There many reasons that churches have for being "baptized" in water. I would like to suggest some good reasons. It is a tradition that helps one identify with the local body of believers. It is a symbol of a new life. It gives the one being baptized an opportunity to profess his faith publicly. Baptism in water is something that lets the local congregation know that the one being baptized is on the same page with our local church's vision. These are good reasons to be baptized in water. It would be confusing for the participant to get baptized in water because, "If I don't I'll be sinning or disobeying". Or, "I'm not saved until I get baptized in water". Or on the contrary, "I not ready to commit". Not ready to commit? I've heard this. You think you're "saved" but not ready to commit? Lots of problems there. So I guess the real question is, "Why wouldn't you get water baptized in water for the right reason"? It's a public way of saying "I agree" with this body of believers". But it's not required anymore than keeping God's diet. Pigs still aren't clean. But, abstaining from eating pigs is not required. Well, unless you want to be healthy. It is the Maker's Diet.

Acts 11

A REPEAT. AS IF WE needed to hear the whole thing again because we tend to get things mixed up. Peter emphasizes again that the vision from God was about people not animals and creeping things. It was about salvation, the baptism Jesus baptizes with, in the Spirit, for the ethnos, the Gentiles. God granted repentance to life to everyone, to the nations. Being baptized in the Spirit, the Holy Spirit, is life and it is a gift to everyone. It is a new life and that by grace, you are saved by grace. All we do is receive it. But we must receive it. God forces no one. He neither forces to receive the gift nor forces to go to hell. We have a choice to be rescued or not. Because we are naturally totally depraved and have nothing good in us before being cleansed, the most common reason for receiving salvation is being scared of going to hell. It is totally selfish. But God already knew that and provided for us anyway. Why wouldn't someone receive eternal life? Probably haven't hit bottom yet. Like an addict, we have to hit bottom and realize we need help. Well, what about kids? Some kids receive salvation at Sunday school. When we become men and women, we put away childish things and think like adults. Some carry their salvation through to adulthood. Some don't. Some need to experience salvation as an adult. "But I thought it was *eternal* life"? I know. But sometimes the salvation experience of the caterpillar doesn't transfer to the butterfly. "Why?" Don't know. The child doesn't automatically become the adult. Well, maybe physically, but there's a lot of boys and girls out there in grown up bodies.

Many Gentiles were turning to the Lord, so the apostles sent Barnabas to exhort them all to stay near the Lord. A lot of people were being saved so Barnabas went to Tarsus to get Saul/Paul and together they taught for a whole year in Antioch and they began to be called, "Christians".

Acts 12

KING HEROD, AN EDOMITE, an Idomean, a descendant of Esau and not an Israelite at all, but called a Jew, killed James, the brother of John, with a sword. We see the word "Jew" and have certain ideas about what kind of person this is. Some think it's a religion. Some think it's a race, or both. Some think of Mediterranean, Mid-eastern looking people and some think of people from Russia, very white. Some think of Hitler's Germany. Whatever the case, "Jews" means different things to different people. The Jews of the book of Acts is also confusing. In the time of Esther, in all one hundred twenty seven provinces of Persia, from India to Ethiopia, many of the people of the land "became" Jews! (Est 8:17). These were not ethnic Jews descended from Judah, Jacob's (Israel's) son. In Israel the Edomites, descendants of Esau in the South became "Jews" during the time between Malachi and Matthew. These are Jews who say they are Jews but are not, but are the synagogue of Satan (Rev 2:9). Esau was Jacob's brother who sold his birthright and found no place of repentance (Heb 12:16). Also, there were those who intermarried with the Babylonians and were a mixed breed much like the Samaritans. This is why Saul/Paul had such a hard time with the "Jews". They were not God's chosen people. They were the leaders and ringleaders, high priests and rulers among the people. Paul later wrote that these "Jews" were "those who killed the Lord Jesus and their own prophets........being contrary to all men" (1 Thes 2:15). This was Herod. A killer, not a real "Jew". Since Cain killed Abel the killing hasn't ceased, until Jesus reigns. Herod then goes after Peter. Around Passover, he was locked up. It's interesting this year, 2016, that we have the holiday of "Easter" which is supposed to be the resurrection of Jesus a whole month before Passover, when Jesus was killed and buried. So this year Jesus raises from the dead a whole month before he dies. And we wonder why people are confused? Just explain to me how a chocolate bunny lays painted eggs that hatch into marshmallow chicks. Okay, so the feast of Astarte, (Easter), the pagan goddess, was long before the resurrection of Jesus. She was a fertility goddess and was celebrated with fertility symbols, such as rabbits and eggs and chicks in the spring. We should be celebrating his death and resurrection, i.e. Passover and Firstfruits, two feasts of the Lord. We don't have to. It's not required but if you want a day to celebrate, just sayin'. Keep it real.

Peter thought he saw a vision but an angel really did release him from prison. The others had a hard time believing also. Rhoda tells them," Peter's at the door" and they tell her she's insane. Well, after all, she was just the servant girl, revelations should come from highly decorated scholars and theologians right?

Barnabas still has Saul/Paul and adds John Mark to the entourage.

Acts 13

S O OFF THEY GO, Barnabas, Paul and Mark as a helper, travelling and preaching in the synagogues. They encounter a false Jewish prophet, a conjurer, named Elymas (Barjesus). He tries to keep the procounsul, Sergius Paulus from listening to Paul. Paul, who was Saul, was an enemy of the Lord and a son of the Devil before he was born of the Spirit, like all of us, and was blinded. Paul calls this one an enemy and a son of the Devil and tells him he will be blind. And he was. When the proconsul saw this he believed and was astounded. John Mark leaves and goes back to Jerusalem. Paul preaches in the synagogue and gets to the part about David being a "man after God's own heart". Now there's a phrase. We use it. But what did it mean? It's used to "prove" that even though David had God's heart, he still committed adultery and murder. Confusing! What does it mean? Simply put, it means that the people wanted a king like the other nations. (The beginning of every temptation begins with, "I want something different than what God wants "God's heart"). God said, "No". The people rebelled. You can read the story in 1 Samuel 8. God said, "They have rejected me"! They chose Saul the son of Kish. Bad idea. Not God's heart. Not God's choosing. Later, God chose David. God's heart, God's choosing. A man after God's own heart only means that God chose him (1 Sam 13:14). David was not born of the Spirit. David did not have God's heart. No one did until Jesus rose from the dead. That's why the OLD testament says, "The heart is deceitful above all things and it is incurable; who can know it?" (Jer 17:9). A new heart is clean. David's prayer was create in me a clean heart. A born from above heart (center) and a new spirit is not deceitful and is the cure. A man after God's own heart simply means God chose him instead of the people's heart choosing him. Let's not make a doctrine of "I'm just a sinner like David but I'm after (like chasing) God's heart. Being a God chaser might sound cool but it's God that chases us. He's the one who plants seed after seed trying to get us to receive and bear fruit. We hear and don't bear fruit at different stages of our lives like the sidewalk and the stony ground and the thorns, but finally when the ground is broken up and fertile we receive his salvation and bear fruit (Mt 13:3-24). God pursues us. Then we become a man or woman with God's heart. And the hand that stole, steals no more (Eph 4:28); Fruit! "I didn't change at all, but I thought I was saved". And there's no change? Try again. God is trying again and again and again until we bear fruit of the Spirit. "You MUST be BORN of the Spirit!" Not just conceived. Not just a seed planted, but full term, born. Spiritually speaking, there are abortions and miscarriages or the seed just doesn't stick for some reason and the pregnancy is interrupted. Maybe the birds stole the seed. Maybe the roots weren't deep enough. Maybe the thorns choked it. The point is God doesn't stop planting, trying, pursuing. He is choosing us with his own heart and we become born of the Spirit and bear fruit of the Spirit because He chooses us. We just receive. That's all. You can't work for it, repent for it or be baptized for it; it's a gift. "Receive the Spirit", God is breathing into you.

Luke is writing this, who (probably) also wrote the gospel according to Luke before this which includes the "virgin birth"(Lk 1:30-32). This is where the angel says that Jesus will be given the throne of his "father" David. The angel knew that Joseph was not the "father" of Jesus and therefore neither was David. "But", some say, "yeah, but he was of Mary's egg". What? So it was the sperm of the Holy Spirit and the egg of Mary? See what thinking physical does? That's just creepy and wrong. God planted a seed, a whole seed, in Mary by the Holy Spirit and she became a surrogate mother only. (please do a search on the internet about what actually happens with a surrogate mother). Jesus was born of a woman. That's all. Whether Paul new of the virgin birth by this time of writing or Luke takes it upon himself to correct the idea of "according to the flesh", as in Romans 1:3 is not clear. Romans was written first then Luke and then Acts. So when Paul wrote Romans he didn't know about the virgin birth; it's possible that Luke told him about it when rewriting the events of the book of Acts thirty years after they occurred. Luke goes on to quote Paul, "Of the seed (God's seed) of this one, according to promise (not flesh), God raised up a savior to Israel, Jesus (and obviously, now, to every nation; but Paul didn't know that either).

Interestingly, we will not find anywhere in the book of Acts, nor the any of the epistles that Jesus was born without a human father. No one talks about a "virgin birth". It wasn't required to become born of the Spirit. To believe in the resurrection was required but not the birth. For years, thirty or forty years, until Matthew and Luke were written no one spoke or wrote of a "virgin birth" let alone require that one believe it to become born of the Spirit. Why is it required now? I believe it, but his death and resurrection paid for our punishment, not his birth. We should be proclaiming his death (and resurrection) until he comes (1Cor 11:26). In popularity, his birth has replaced the Resurrection with all the "Christmas" festivities, "the most wonderful time of the year". Paul continues, "John going before to proclaim, before his coming, a baptism of repentance to all the people of Israel", to proclaim, to announce that a baptism of repentance was coming, a baptism of Spirit was coming. John's baptism was water and it didn't cleanse anyone. He only proclaimed that the cleansing was coming. Jesus will give us redemption, salvation and mercy (Luke 1:68-75). Then in verse 76 of Lk 1, John will prepare and give "knowledge" of salvation and forgiveness and mercy.

Paul preaches resurrection, "But God raised him up"!(verse 30). The Jews seeing the crowds were jealous and contradicted Paul, because that's what jealousy does. Paul said, "We're turning to the Gentiles". But.......(we have a chapter break).........

Acts 14

OKAY, NOW WE CAN continue, remember there were no breaks in the original writings. Chapter 14 starts with, "and" Paul and Barnabas were back in the synagogues in Iconium and speaking to both Jews and Gentiles. The Jews caused trouble again and tried to stone them even though miracles were occurring. They flee to Lystra. Paul and Barnabas encounter a man who has been lame from birth and Paul tells him to stand up. A miracle occurs. The man leaps up and walks. The people say, "The gods have come down to us becoming like men". Upon first reading this, many would think, "Well, that's dumb; gods don't come down and become men"! Yet, they have no trouble saying that God came down and became a man. "But Jesus is different; God became man." No. God was IN Christ. "Okay, so why focus on that? Why make a big deal about that? What difference does it make? Because to worship the flesh of Jesus, as God, is idolatry. God is Spirit, the Spirit of Jesus, the Holy Spirit. Eternal life is to know the ONLY true God and Jesus Christ whom he has sent. Paul and Barnabas were not gods. They didn't think they were gods; they said they were men and pointed their attention to the living God from whom all good things come. The words Paul spoke are Paul's words not God's words nor Hermes' words. Paul made it clear that he is a man just like them. Paul's spirit is not God. The Holy Spirit (God) bears witness with Paul's spirit that he is A son of God, not THE only begotten Son of God. Jesus' Spirit is God, the fullness of God! When Jesus speaks, God is speaking. The man, named Jesus didn't become God, but the Spirit whose name is Jesus (God) made himself a body to dwell in. Just because the man's name is Jesus doesn't make flesh God. There would be many of God in Mexico if that were the case, because there are a lot of men named "Jesus".

Then here come the Jews again, following, persuading the crowds and stoning Paul until they thought he was dead. They left him for dead, and he may have died, but the disciples surrounded him and arising he entered the city. Whether dead or presumed dead by stoning, this man was in critical condition. And the text says, "arising". He just got up and went to the city. And the next day preached the gospel and made many disciples. What? Looking like a Zombie? Probably not. The disciples probably prayed and asked God to raise him up. Either way dead or critically injured, a miracle took place and Paul was restored to health and continued to preach the "gospel", the resurrection of Jesus Christ. All this is taking place just a few years after Jesus ascended. But nothing was written yet. Whether Paul was remembering this to Luke (or whoever is writing the "Acts"; we'll just refer to the author of Acts and Luke as Luke) and he was taking dictation, or Luke was remembering being with Paul and hearing these stories earlier, we can't be sure. But it was written after Luke wrote "Luke" which was thirty or forty years after these things happened. So remembering stories we tend to leave some things out and focus on the purpose of the writing which in this case was "preaching the gospel" which was the resurrection of Jesus, the man Christ Jesus. God didn't need to be resurrected because God didn't die. God is life and cannot die. Jesus, the man, died and was raised from the dead. Jesus the Spirit didn't die but left the body and went back to the omnipresent God, whose name is Jesus. Jesus the Spirit raised the body of Jesus the man.

Acts 15

INTERESTING. SOME WERE TEACHING that if you're not circumcised you can't be saved. Whoa, imagine the implications today! What about the women? I'll bet Christianity wouldn't be so popular if that were the case. Thankfully, there is nothing we can do to earn salvation. There is nothing we can do to be saved. We can only receive it. He paid for us. No one else could have paid for us. Jesus of Nazareth (really of Bethlehem) born of a woman but without original sin is the only man that could have taken our punishment. Everyone else is a descendant of Adam and would have sin and it had to be a man, not a spirit, nor an angel or any other creature. He who knew no sin became sin. By one man sin entered the world but the gift of salvation by grace is of the one man, Jesus Christ (Rom 5:12-15 paraphrase). They called him the son of Joseph and the son of David because they thought he was. They called him Jesus of Nazareth because they thought he was. Nathaniel was like, "Can anything good come out of Nazareth"? They even argued about it in John chapter 7:41:ff, "The Christ is from Bethlehem", because they thought Jesus was from Galilee," so he can't be the Messiah". The Pharisees said, ".......a prophet has not been raised from Galilee". (Jonah was. But I guess they forgot. And the only sign given to them was the sign of Jonah!). So some religious leaders were putting restrictions and rules and regulations and requirements on the people. Imagine that! And every denomination, even the denomination called "non-denominational" has their rules. There are no rules. Receive the Spirit!!!

Interesting again. Paul caused Timothy to get circumcised when he was going to preach to the Jews, (Acts 16:1-5) because although Timothy's mother and grandmother were Jewish and raised Timothy in the Jewish scriptures (2 Tim 3:15) his father was a Greek. So he "required" Timothy to get circumcised to be like them, (I guess they examined people, creepy) but later had a big fight with Peter because Peter wouldn't eat with the Gentiles when the Jews were around to be like them and called him a hypocrite. Funny how we can see the "wrong" other people do and can't see the same thing in ourselves, like a beam in our eye or something.

The term which means "not a little" in Greek is what was used to mean "huge". A huge discussion, dissention, disputation, and discord broke out between Paul and Barnabas and the "Judah-izers". This first attempt at "Messianic Judaism" was started by the Pharisees who had to have rules to follow and be legal about everything. They said it was necessary to tell new believers, real born of the Spirit Christians that they had to keep the law of Moses including circumcision. Later Paul would call them dogs and tell us to beware of them (Phi'p 3:2). The sign of the new covenant is "circumcision of the heart" not the flesh, and is evidenced by fruit, good fruit, lasting fruit, fruit of the Spirit, love, not the emotion "love" but spiritual love, a change of heart and a change of behavior.

There is nothing that we can do to be accepted by God as his son or daughter and there is nothing we can do after receiving the Spirit to become any more or less accepted by God. We have modern day "Judah-izers" telling us we have to do things the way their church does it or we are disobeying God and are in sin. Make no mistake, our sins are gone and there is no more judgment (Jn 5:24). "What about the judgment seat of Christ?" There is no more judgment for believers. I've been judged at the judgment seat of Christ and been found guilty. I was guilty, convicted, sentenced and put on death row. I deserved death. Then Jesus took my place. My sentence has been served. And yours has too! It is finished. Peter agrees. Acts 15:10, grace and belief. That's all. But, James and the others heard what they thought Jesus meant. So he gave them a few rules which we no longer keep. Why? because like drawing straws and going to the temple (or church on Sunday) at the hour of prayer, or not eating certain foods or water baptism or grape juice and crackers, nothing, NOTHING, is required except belief. So they told them to abstain from "things sacrificed to idols, and blood and strangled and fornication, which we thought "seemed" good to the Holy Spirit. I keep the food laws in Lev 11, because I want to be healthy, I've been baptized in water 4 times because I wanted to identify with the local body of believers and I take "communion" every time it's offered. I go to church on Sunday. But none of this is required to become born of the Spirit or to grow in the Spirit or to be right with God. I give money, and I think ten percent is a good guide to go by, but it's not required, and God's not going to throw lightning rods at you if you don't and your crops won't die. You won't win the lottery if you do either. That's old covenant thinking. But it is more blessed to give than to receive. The point is: the new covenant is on the inside and shows up on the outside. Nothing we can do on the outside will change the inside. They found this out. Later. But for now in Acts 15, well, they were still trying to put new wine in old wineskins. Never a good idea. The new believers rejoiced and were relieved that getting "cut" was no longer a ritual, to belong; the other rituals they could accept.

When Paul in Acts 9 was still Saul, he came to the apostles and they feared him. Barnabas stood up for him. Barnabas is now standing up for John Mark but Paul is still mad at him for leaving them in 13:13. There was a sharp contention between Paul and Barnabas and they separated from each other. Sad. It happens. Barnabas took John Mark, Paul took Silas. Who was right? It didn't matter. Good things were done by both, but we should be able to reconcile. Separation and isolation hurt. We should always look for reconciliation. Sometimes we have to wait for the other person to come around. And like many fights in relationships, we forget what the issue was but just know that the other person was wrong, or so it seemed to us. This happens in church? With brothers and sisters in the Lord? You know it does, it's probably happened to you. If not it will. What can we do? Forgive and reconcile. And obviously, just because God is using us to preach or even doing miracles, it doesn't mean God approves of our thinking or attitude. He approves of who we are, his children, but that's because of what he's done.

When we are born of the Spirit, born from above, saved, a new creature in Christ, we have a new spirit. We don't get a new body, yet; we don't get a new soul (mind, will, emotions). We become "spiritual" sons and daughters, children, of God. So God approves of us, who we are, spirit, but doesn't always approve of what we do. He paid for that and that payment continues to pay for our sins, present and future. Time and space do not restrict God. However, our response to receiving this most wonderful, free gift should cause us to change in soul and eventually body as our attitude and behavior changes. The tree should bear fruit. Good fruit. Paul and Barnabas and Peter and all of the "new testament" writers had issues and faults and sin to overcome in soul and body. Their writings reflect this sometimes. The words Jesus spoke however, are SPIRIT and life. The words Jesus spoke are perfect, the Word of God, because Jesus is the Word of God. He had no sin. His body and soul were from heaven not a descendant from earthy Adam. That's why we should take Jesus' words as "gospel" and the others only when they agree with Jesus. The writers contradict themselves and each other, but God never contradicts himself and Jesus is God...... in SPIRIT! The spirit in the body of Jesus Christ is God, and his body and soul were made in heaven. Reducing his body to a single cell and planting it in Mary caused his body to become mortal because he allowed it to be born of a woman to "dwell" among us. God never became flesh. The Word did not "become" flesh; the Greek word there is "birthed" not "become" (not 1096. ginomai, but 1079 genete in Strong's dictionary, the same as the verse before referring to people being "born" of God, Jn 1:13-14). Jesus said, "That which is born of spirit is spirit and that which is born of flesh is flesh". God is spirit. The body he made for himself is flesh.

God's name is Jesus, the name above all names (at least in English, Yeshua in Hebrew). Christ is the Greek translation of Messiah which is Hebrew and in English means the anointed one, a man. Jesus is the spirit, (but is also the man's name, like many in Mexico but that doesn't make them God). Christ is the man. God is spirit. His body is man. God was in Christ reconciling the world unto himself (2 Cor 5:19). Jesus said, after his resurrection, "Touch me..........a spirit does not have flesh and bones as you see me having". Spirit is never flesh. Spirit never becomes flesh. Spirit is IN flesh, like a tent, a tabernacle, a dwelling. He dwelled among us. God is not a man, never has been man and never will be man. God is spirit, the Holy Spirit. The Son, who is eternal, is Spirit, the Holy Spirit of Jesus, but confined, being limited in a man, the man, Christ Jesus, the only mediator between God and man (1 Tim 2:5). The name of the Father is Jesus, the name of the Son is Jesus, he came in his father's name (Jn 5:43). To know him, the ONLY true God and Jesus Christ (God in a man) whom he has sent, this IS eternal life! (Jn 17:3). The Son in the body learned. Father already knows everything (omniscient). But in the body, the Son was limited. The Son could not be in two places at the same time. Father is omnipresent, able to be everywhere at the same time. Father is all powerful or omnipotent, but the Son in a body was limited and "could not" do many works of power because of their unbelief (Matt 13:58). The Father and Son are one. One Spirit. The Holy Spirit. The man Christ Jesus is a man (the body Father created for himself) with the fulness of God dwelling in him. We are children of God with only a small deposit of the Spirit dwelling within us and the Holy Spirit bears witness with our spirit that we are the sons and daughters of God (Col 2:9, Rom 8: all, but especially 16). Please look these passages up and read them.

In verse 22 there's a lot of "it seemed good" going on. I think this only illustrates more how the leaders of the church were men, not gods trying to do the right thing. They made mistakes and spoke and wrote how they felt and believed at the time like Paul and Barnabas explained in 14:15, "We're just like you, we have feelings and speak and write what we think, we're not gods". Yet some, dare I say most Christians want to believe that Paul's writings are "God Breathed". The scriptures, the TaNaKh, the old testament writings are God Breathed. The word of God was written by the prophets and is now spoken by Jesus. The rest of the new testament writings are a written account of how the apostles understood what they thought Jesus meant.

Take Romans chapters 9,10 and 11. Paul is pouring his heart out about how he feels. He is writing "his conscience", not God's dictates. He has never ending pain and he is grieving and his grief is great. He could wish himself to be a curse from Christ! That's not God speaking!

We could understand the Bible so much clearer if we understood these were just letters that the apostles wrote trying to understand Jesus' words and trying to piece it all together. They are not gods! He is troubled about his brothers in the flesh. He gives many examples of "scriptures" pulled out of context and coupled with others to try to soothe his grief. I wouldn't suggest that we try to make doctrine based on these chapters. But some do. And by the way we haven't been grafted into anything. That was Paul's analogy. We are BORN! not adopted, not grafted. Jesus said, "You must be born". I love Paul and I love his rants and reasonings but even Peter said Paul's writings were hard to understand. We're not going to skim over his writings and get it. It takes study and diligence and research and putting Jesus' words first.

So it "seemed good" in verse 22 and it "seemed good" in verse 25 and then it "seemed good" to the Holy Spirit? What? And to us? What? Now the Holy Spirit is putting these restrictions on the Gentiles? Well it may have seemed right to them at the time. But it doesn't seem right now and I seriously doubt that the Holy Spirit had anything to do with it. It's okay. God's word is infallible. The words of the Prophets and the words of Jesus are infallible. But the rest of it is "What they thought he meant". And there's nothing wrong with that unless we are trying to make gods out of them. It "seemed good" again in verse 34. Notice they weren't saying, God said.

Then the big fight breaks out. Barnabas wants to give Mark a second chance. Paul is adamant, "no". They separate. Barnabas helps Mark, and Paul who got a second chance through Barnabas would rather take Silas. Bad people? No. Just people. These men are just men. We need to get this idea out of our heads that they only thought "God's thoughts". These men were fallible. Paul said, "His ways are past finding out" (Rom 11:33). Their writings are fallible. Heaven and Earth may pass away but the words of Jesus in the original manuscripts will never pass away, not the words of Paul......or Peter.....James.....John. They are in the Bible and we should read them but never make a doctrine of something that Jesus didn't say. And we better make sure that what we think Jesus said, IS what he said.

Acts 16

P AUL WILL WRITE IN Galatians later that he was right to stand up to Peter and opposed him to his face because he was to be blamed, concerning eating with the Gentiles (Gal 2:11ff) when the Jews weren't around and then not eating with them when the Jews showed up. And most commentators jump to confusions by agreeing with Paul, calling Peter a hypocrite. Wow, so, Paul's writings are supposedly God speaking and Peter, well, he's just a hypocrite? No. Both men were writing and practicing what they thought Jesus meant. It "seemed good" at the time. But look at this blatant example of Paul doing the exact same thing of which he accused Peter. Paul took Timothy and circumcised him in the flesh to reach the Jews! Personally I would find this a bit more appalling. Paul had this idea that he ".....become all things to all men that he may save some" (1 Cor 9:19-23). This is exactly what Peter had done but Paul just knew he was right and Peter was wrong. They were just men. They were not gods. Jesus is God. His words are God speaking. The rest, well, if it agrees with Jesus then yes, but pointing out other people's sin and hypocrisy is not. Paul should have removed the plank from his own eye instead of looking at the splinter in Peter's eye. This is history, not judgment. I am in no position to judge Paul, nor anyone else, however, a spiritual person judges all things (not people, but still judges).

The point is we are reading history according to Luke, according to Paul's dictation and it is a good description of what was going on. Acts is not a prescription! If you think it is we can circumcise those of you who want to reach the Jews..........That's what I thought.

This is where we find that Timothy's father was a Greek. His grandmother, Lois and his mother, Eunice brought him up in the "scriptures" from a babe, and of course the only "scriptures" then were the TaNaKh, or what we call the old testament books (2 Tim 1:5, 3:15-16). So, speaking of the "scriptures" that Timothy learned, Paul writes that they are all inspired by God. Context makes a difference. All scripture then, means all of the TaNaKh according to Paul. None of the new testament had been written and distributed yet. "What about Peter calling Paul's writings "scripture"? Yeah, about that, let's look at what Peter said. Peter said, "Paul wrote to you.......in all his letters,.......which the unlearned and unsettled pervert as also they do the remaining (Strong's 3062, 3063, left over, remaining) "scriptures". The only "scriptures" they had that remained were the TaNaKh. This verse, one verse, out of context, has been used to mean that Paul's letters are like the "other" scriptures therefore whatever Paul wrote is scripture and also stretched out to mean that the whole of the new testament books is "Scripture". The word is "remaining" not "other" which agrees with the context of the whole of the New Testament. None of the New Testament "books" are "scripture". We have words of Jesus, which is the Word of God. We have the gospels which is the good news about the resurrection. And we have letters from the apostles that were written with the mind of what "seemed good" to them. They disagreed with each other and blamed each other. That's not the word of God. It's history. It's accurate history. And there are examples to follow and some to not follow. God's word never contradicts itself. The word "Scripture" always applies to the Old Testament books only. Please look it up.

So Paul and the newly circumcised Timothy are now going through the cities telling the Gentiles that they need to "keep the decrees having been determined by the apostles and the elders in Jerusalem". Still want this to be a prescription? The churches grew stronger and in number anyway. A big church is no indication that what is being taught is what Jesus meant. People don't grow people; God grows people. And God looks at the heart not the performance. When Paul has a vision to go to Macedonia, Luke includes himself, "we". This is where Paul and Timothy and Silas and now Luke meet the women who met at the river to pray led by Lydia, a successful business woman and prayer warrior. Enter the demon possessed woman who "brought much gain to her lords". Paul calls the demon out, but they get arrested and beaten with sticks with many wounds and imprisoned. This is what it meant to be a leader in the "Church" in Paul's day, arrested, beat and imprisoned, no stages, no elaborate hotel conferences, no cars and jets and rock star performances. "Christianity" has become popular and fashionable. Jesus said, "The world will hate you, for it hated me"(Jn 15:18-20, 17:14). All the apostles were martyred except John and he was exiled to a remote island and then possibly martyred. The happy ending is they all spend eternity with Jesus. "What are we going to do for eternity? Clouds and harps and sing the same verse over and over?" I don't know the future; no one does. What I do know is that there are billions of solar systems in each of the billions of galaxies that we know now. What if God wanted to populate every planet in every solar system in every galaxy? That would take a while! We might be very busy traveling for light years.......without the star wars.

There shall be no end.

Paul and Silas are miraculously released from prison and the jailer wanted to know what he could do to be saved. Paul said, "Believe on the Lord Jesus Christ". That's it. That's how people get "saved". After they were saved they followed tradition and got baptized in water. Notice that water baptism was not a prerequisite to get saved nor a requirement to stay saved.

Acts 17

P AUL AGAIN PREACHING TO the Jews in the synagogues from the "Scriptures" (that would be the Jewish Bible, the TaNaKh), on the sabbath days, about the resurrection of the Christ and that the Christ is Jesus (Jesus of Nazareth). And again the Jews are disobeying and causing turmoil. Off to another synagogue (all this after Paul said he would turn to the Gentiles; it was a struggle for him), to Berea. These Jews received the word because they examined the TaNaKh (Scriptures) daily. Many believed and also Greeks, but here come the bad Jews again stirring up trouble. They send Paul to Athens and Paul sends for Silas and Timothy to join him. Paul is already back in the synagogue. In 13:46 Paul said, "We turn to the Gentiles" and said that the Jews were not worthy of eternal life and quoted a "scripture" from Isaiah 49:6, but he didn't mean it. Evidently. In the market place Paul preached the Resurrection of Jesus, because that's the power we've been given. Paul explains that God cannot be contained in a temple made by man's hands but is creator. He also explains that God anointed a man to be raised from the dead, speaking of Jesus. Christ is a man. God is a Spirit. God was in Christ. (2 Cor 5:19, Jn 4:24)

Acts 18

I N CORINTH, PAUL MEETS Aquila and Priscilla, both Jews and fellow tentmakers. He lived and worked with them. It's okay to have a job and earn money to support your ministry. Not everyone can get paid to "do ministry". Paul didn't. Jesus didn't. Where'd we get this idea? That being said there are CEO's of businesses called churches that have to go to meetings and make decisions, especially in larger congregations that require organization. This is a job and they should get paid. I just wouldn't suggest paying someone to pray for me. In a church where is was counseling, I received compensation for the time I was missing on my job, so that I could have time to counsel. Some would say that I was paid to counsel, so now I just give my time.

Paul again enters the synagogues to preach. Again he says, "From now on I will go to the Gentiles". He goes to the house next door where the synagogue ruler gets saved. Again, the ruler believed first and then followed the ritual of water baptism. Paul stayed a year and a half teaching them. And again the Jews attack Paul. Eventually Paul leaves for Syria with Priscilla and Aquila. Paul again trying to be like the Jews, doing the same thing he withstood Peter to his face about (because "He was to be blamed"), shaves his head, a Jewish thing. He goes to Ephesus and where does he go? To the synagogue and tried to "reason" with the Jews.......again, after announcing twice that he is turning to the Gentiles. Paul is not a bad person. He loves his race. But he is human, he is not God and the things he says and writes are not always God speaking. He leaves and goes to a Jewish feast in Jerusalem. If we refuse to see that Paul and the other epistle writers were just men inspired by God to write things, but in their own flawed personalities, then we will have to think that the word of God is flawed, which it is not.

The concern some have is where do you then draw the line? Were Jesus' words recorded correctly? The recorded words of Jesus in Matthew, Mark, Luke and John in the original manuscripts all agree and are consistent with each other and consistent with the character of Jesus. I believe that the recorded words of Jesus are Spirit and the Word of God. I believe the man Christ is divine in that he was neither of Joseph's seed nor Mary's egg, but he was a man, not a God-man. God, the fullness of God was in him. He is the only one in which the only begotten of the Father lives. I say that to make a clear distinction between the words of Jesus and the words of the apostles who said what they thought Jesus meant. As flawed as they might have been, I think if they could see what the "church" has turned into, they would think they failed in some way.

Apollos was Jewish. He taught the Scriptures. Scriptures are Jewish, the old testament. He understood only the baptism of John. Jewish. Priscilla and Aquila expounded the way of God more accurately to him. Yup, a woman was teaching a man. Apollos upon hearing about Jesus goes to the Jews publicly and proves through the Scriptures, the Hebrew Bible, the TaNaKh that Jesus is the Messiah.

Acts 19

THIS IS REALLY SIMPLE language. Why it gets so tangled up so quickly amazes me. But if you have your own denominational agenda to push, you can twist things to mean something they were never intended to mean. We find that at the same time that Apollos is getting a clue from a woman and her husband, Paul is trekking to Ephesus and finds about twelve disciples. Disciples? of whom? He said to them, "Did you receive the Holy Spirit believing"? They said, "We didn't hear if there is a Holy Spirit". Again, this raises the question, "Who's disciples were they"? Then Paul says, "To what, then were you baptized"? And they said, "The baptism of John". Now John's baptism, the baptism of water, never saved anybody; it only paved the way for repentance in the Messiah which was coming. Paul explained that John pointed to Christ Jesus to believe in. Hearing this they were baptized (not in water again) but into the NAME of the Lord Jesus, Paul laying hands on them, the Holy Spirit came on them (baptism in Spirit). They spoke in languages and prophesied, or spoke of the great deeds of God (just like chapter 2). Baptism in the Spirit in those days gave the baptized the ability to speak languages of others supernaturally without learning the language. This helped "jump start" the spread of the gospel. Simple. The gifts of the Spirit were never meant to look like a three ring circus, then nor now.

Paul went to the synagogue again! For three months he "reasoned" with them. He managed to get some disciples and took them with him when he departed from the hardened Jews who spoke evil of "The Way" (the name of the "Church" at that time). For two years Paul taught both Jews and Greeks. God blessed Paul with uncommon works, miracles to heal and cause evil spirits to leave people and give them a sound mind. Some tried to copycat but it didn't work. When the people realized that all the magical, incantations and superstitious rituals didn't do anything they burned their books and trusted in the word of the Lord. We would be wise to do the same thing. There are too many books with too many formulas and rituals. Even this book would be unnecessary if there were no other commentary. The only purpose this book serves is to get us to look at the word of God, words of Jesus without someone telling us what Jesus meant. The Spirit does that! The purpose of this book is to cast down imaginations that men have dreamed up (religion, denominations, rituals and superstitions) and forced us to believe for fear of being "cast out of the synagogue". I value the fellowship of the saints, but not at the cost of forfeiting the truth, obviously.

Paul desired to go to Jerusalem and then to Rome, but he stayed in Asia for "a time". There was a violent uprising because Paul had messed with their income. They were making money off of their religion and Paul preaching the resurrection of Jesus and salvation in him alone, caused people to trust the word of God and no other. Remember, they burned their books. They weren't buying more. "Christian" merchandising has reached billions. What would happen if someone said we don't need all that, just the Bible and we can meet in homes. There would be an uprising. First, they would have to discredit the one saying read the Bible without commentary or books. It would have to be more subtle today. The worst part of deception is we don't know. But you can trust the red words. "Well, Glenn, what if people did burn their books and read only the Bible and placed Jesus words first and burned your book too"? Smile. Success. I would have fulfilled what I think my mission is.

Acts 20

PAUL SPENDS THREE MONTHS in Greece and then......the Jews are after him again. So he desired to go through Macedonia and a bunch of men joined him. Then Luke includes himself again saying "us" and "we". Getting ready to leave the next day Paul preached until midnight and some young man fell asleep because of the longwinded speech Paul was giving and fell out the third story window. He died. But Paul fell on him and said, "His soul is in him". What happened there? He was raised from the dead. This wasn't CPR. This was a big deal! It simply says, "They brought the boy alive". But he was dead. Imagine if this was your boy. This was miraculous. Imagine if this happened at your church. It would be all over the news, tv, internet.... viral. But here it's just simply mentioned as a matter of fact. Why? Because they didn't base their beliefs on miracles. Everything Paul says must be God speaking because Paul's hankie healed people and he raised the dead, right? Wrong. If what Paul says or anyone else says agrees with what Jesus said then God is speaking. The miracle passed by almost unnoticed; Luke just continues his travelogue, "We set sail for Assos.......". The power to preach is in the resurrection of Jesus, not in miracles signs and wonders. Jesus had said, "I will say, Depart from me, I never knew you" to ones who had performed miracles (Mt 7:23).

Paul took Luke on some travels and then desired to go to Jerusalem for Pentecost. Jewish. Paul recounts all the plots that the Jews have made against him, but he can't stay away from them. Twice, that we know of he said he was through with them. But he still went back and they were still against him. Jesus told the Jews that their "house is left to you desolate"(Mt 23:38) and "The kingdom of God will be taken from you and given to a nation bringing forth the fruits of it"(Mt 21:43). Paul is conflicted about his countrymen and we understand but we need to follow Jesus on this one. We're not grafted into anything and Jews and Greeks are on an even playing field; there is no advantage for the Jew. In Christ there is no difference (Gal 3:28) Paul would write later. "Yes, but Paul said," Yes, that's right, Paul said (Rom 9,10,11). "Jesus said", trumps what Paul said and he's okay with that.

Now Paul is saying that the Holy Spirit is saying go to Jerusalem, being "bound" by the Spirit, really? Does the Spirit force us to do things. (And just because Jesus appears to Paul in a dream and says, "like you did in Jerusalem also do in Rome", doesn't mean he forced him to go to Jerusalem nor Rome. 23:11) Or is this just the way Paul feels? I could understand that. But we have some running around saying, "God told me to............" and God told me to........." ad nauseum. I've even heard, "God told me to eat at McDonald's. In these "last days", God has spoken to us through his Son. God speaks red words. Let's not say, "God said" when God has not said. Somewhere, at sometime Jesus said, "It is more blessed to give than to receive". I believe it even though it's not in the gospels. It is consistent with his character. That's why it's important to know his character.

Acts 21

DECISIONS, DECISIONS. WHAT SHOULD I do? "I think God is telling me to..........". And we make our plans then someone comes along with a "prophecy", "a word", that seems contrary. What to do? Agabus the "prophet" tells Paul that if he goes to Jerusalem he'll be bound by the Jews and delivered to the Gentiles. Well, with all the trouble Paul had with the Jews everywhere he went, it wouldn't take a spiritual giant to predict that he'll have a problem with the Jews. But this one verse is used to "prove" that new testament "prophecy" is prediction. And it's not. Paul was like, "so what? I'm going. The Spirit told me to go. You're telling me the Spirit says 'Don't go'? I'm ready to die for Jesus". Not knowing the "will" of the Lord everyone said, "Let the will of the Lord be done'. We still do that today when we don't know what to do. It's the "Christian" way of saying "whatever". The will of the Lord is that we witness about the resurrection of Jesus. The apostles, led by James are still a Jewish sect, keeping traditions and rituals and laws. They were pleased with all the Jews that had come to Jesus in Jerusalem, but warned Paul that they were against him because they thought he taught against Moses. They suggest he act like a Jew and do all the rituals. What a mess! Yeah, we do that too. Just act like everyone else to fit in. Don't dare have a different thought about the freedom we have in Christ or you'll be thought a heretic and we won't let you fit in. The apostles are still pushing this food law thing as a requirement to be accepted in the church.

The Jews again seize Paul and beat him before the authorities were able to arrest him. And that "Prophecy" wasn't quite right.....He wasn't bound by the Jews, they were going to kill him. He wasn't turned over to the Gentiles, they rescued him and bound him in the process.

Acts 22

FINALLY HE IS ALLOWED to speak in his own defense. He tells his story, especially about his Damascus Road experience only this time Jesus calls himself Jesus the Nazarene. And after all this speech he finally announces that Jesus has sent him to the Gentiles from the beginning. But Paul wanted to reach his own people. And again, his own people want him dead. As they were about to flog him, Paul announced that he was a Roman. The man in charge said he bought his citizenship but Paul was born Roman. So he brought him before the Sanhedrin to speak to them.

Acts 23

P AUL SPEAKS, THEY PUNCH him in the mouth. Paul calls the
high priest a "whitened wall", which I guess was really bad to
call someone, and tells him God is going to punch him. Paul is then
accused of reviling the High Priest. Paul says, My bad, I didn't know.
Then realizing that there were Sadducees and Pharisees in the crowd,
Paul announces that he is accused because he believes in the resurrection
which the Pharisees believe and the Sadducees don't so that they ended
up fighting with each other. Clever. Back to the fortress, but Jesus
appears to him and tells him he said the right things and that he should
testify in Rome also. The Jews again plotted Paul's death, saying that
they would not eat until he was dead. Paul's nephew overheard and
revealed the plot to Paul and to the commander. The commander
knowing Paul to be a Roman called two centurions, two hundred
soldiers, seventy horsemen and two hundred spearmen to bring Paul to
the governor, Felix, in Caesarea, with a letter saying that he was about
to be killed by the Jews. They waited for the accusers to arrive.

Acts 24

THE JEWISH LEADERS CAME with the high priest, Ananias and accused Paul of being a ringleader of the Nazarene Sect. We should be so honored for the enemies of Christ to find enough evidence today for us to be accused of being a ringleader of the Nazarene Sect. Then it was Paul's turn to speak. In one sentence he sums up the Creed to which we should all agree. Paul says, "According to the Way.......so I worship the ancestral God, believing all things according to that having been in the Law and the Prophets, having hope toward God, which these themselves admit, of a resurrection being about to be of the dead, both of just and unjust ones". It seems that Felix heard Paul on and off for two years. Felix's wife being a Jew, and Felix hearing Paul's faith in Christ, Felix was afraid. Paul still bound, he was handed over to Festus, the new governor.

Acts 25

ANOTHER PLOT BY THE Jews to kill Paul by asking that he be sent to Jerusalem. Festus said no, he stays in Caesarea. Paul defends himself and Festus doesn't know what to do and Paul appeals to Caesar. Festus agrees. King Agrippa arrives and Festus briefs him saying that all the Jews seem to be accusing him of is their own demon-worship and that Paul says Jesus is alive. Festus then says I'm sending him to Augustus Caesar. But Agrippa says, "I would like to hear him". Festus says, "Tomorrow you shall hear him".

Acts 26

AGRIPPA SAID TO PAUL, "Speak". Paul lays it all out for him and "almost" persuades him to become a follower of Christ. Agrippa with Bernice and speaking to Festus says, "This man does nothing worthy of death nor bonds" and if he hadn't appealed to Caesar he'd be free to go.

Acts 27

W E HAVE A REFERENCE to Luke in that he says "us" when referring to who was on the ship. Luke continues his travelogue. Paul warned them not to sail. But they do and a huge storm, probably a hurricane, beats against the ship and they all thought they would die. Paul reassures them saying, "An angel told me, Do not fear, Paul, you must stand before Caesar and behold God has granted to you all those sailing with you". Then after fourteen days of fasting, some of the men decided to get into a lifeboat pretending to let down an anchor. But Paul told those in charge unless they all stay on the ship, you cannot be saved. So they cut the lifeboat down. Paul then told them to eat. The ship crashed into the sand and was broken but everyone was saved on land.

Acts 28

T HEY WERE WELCOMED ON the island. Well, until they saw a snake bite Paul. They reasoned that he must be a murderer. But he didn't die as they expected so they thought he was a god. Here we go again with men being god. The father of Publius, the chief of this island called Melita, was sick and Paul cured him. The rest who were sick also came to Paul and they were all healed. When it was time to leave the islanders gave the apostles what they needed. All this traveling being done while Paul, in chains, a prisoner is escorted to Rome. In Rome he makes his defense to the chief Jews. They tell him, "All we know is that this sect is spoken against everywhere".

"Christianity" is popular now. What if it wasn't? Or does that send up some kind of red flag that we may not be the same sect that the early apostles were? Paul said, "All that live a godly life in Christ Jesus will suffer persecution" (2 Tim 3:12). Are we? "Well, my coworkers make fun of our traditions". That's it? That's persecution? That's suffering? The early Christians were fed to the lions! I don't think "Christianity" should be so popular, i.e. Christian rock?, Christian comedy, Christian fantasy, Christian fiction? And they're making millions! "Oh, but Glenn, they're spreading the gospel by becoming all things to all men, like Paul said". Somehow I don't think Paul would jump on board with modern "Christianity", and I don't think Jesus would claim it either. I can hear "I never knew you", somewhere in the backround. That doesn't mean that everyone is wrong and going to hell. It just means that I think some of us have moved our compass from true North and we need to be reset. We need to go back to the basics and read Jesus' words without two thousand years of commentary and the world creeping into the "Church". Recently, I spoke to a group of twenty year olds and mentioned "Peter, Paul and Mary". They had never heard of this trio and started guessing about what it could mean. This is a folk group from the "sixties". Only fifty years ago. Things from only fifty years ago are forgotten or twisted. Imagine what can happen in two thousand years if we follow trends and fanciful interpretations meant to be "deep" or "revelation" or just funny to make "the gospel" more interesting, tickling the ears of the congregation. No, I am not saying everybody is wrong. I am saying we need to go back and digest Jesus' words and have our minds renewed and do some spring cleaning and weed out the rituals and distorted superstitions that don't belong in our "faith once delivered to the saints" (Jude 3). Jude says "contending" (which means, with difficulty, to struggle or grapple with, to assert, to argue). Why do we think that is so wrong? We need to argue, that's how we learn and come to agreement. We just need to argue the issue not each other's character flaws.

Finally, Paul caves and agrees with Jesus, "Well did the Holy Spirit speak through Isaiah......"(verse 25, Isa 6:9-10, Mt 13:14). The Jews won't hear. The Gentiles will. There were believing Jews, but they are no better than Gentiles. In Christ there is no difference between Jews and Gentiles. We are not grafted in. We are born of the Spirit! Recently, we had a discussion about how to reach a Muslim. It was said to find a place of agreement first. After much arguing and persuading, we agreed that there is one God. And since we worship God and he (the Muslim) worships God, then we must be worshipping the same God. That was hard to get across, but we agreed with that because of Romans 1, all can understand a God of creation because of creation. The visible reveals the invisible. And we are ALL without excuse. One God. Then we moved along to the God of Abraham, which the Muslim believes also. But Jesus, what about Jesus? They said, "No one comes to the Father except through Jesus" and they don't have Jesus so they are all going to hell. I said, "What about Jews"? They were like, "Well, there are prophecies about Jews being saved". Really? The prophecy is that they will not hear! The point is that we all need a Savior. Jesus said, "Everyone who hears and learns from the Father, comes to me"(Jn 6:45). Therefore, I believe that everyone who has a relationship or worships Father, the God of creation, the God of Abraham upon meeting the "real" Jesus (not a particular denominational Jesus) will love him and receive him, Jew, Muslim or Gentile(Jn 8:42). And if someone lives in a remote part of the world and never meets Jesus or hears the Gospel but worships the God of creation, he will have a chance to meet the real Jesus, in this life or the life to come and he will receive him. "What? That's heresy! If they don't believe like we do here on Earth they're all going to hell!" And I suppose you're the judge now. Jesus came to save, not to judge, why do you? Later Jesus said in John 14:6, that "no one comes to the Father except through me". We can only deduce that those who came to Father and heard him and learned from him were drawn by Jesus, the Spirit of Jesus, the Holy Spirit. That's why Jesus said, "Abraham saw my day and was glad"(Jn 8: 56). The Jews responded with, "You've seen Abraham? You're not even fifty years old yet"! Abraham had a relationship with Father because he was drawn by Jesus. All things were created through Jesus. Time and space didn't restrict him until he became born of a woman. Jesus made visitations as Melchizedek and the "Angel of the Lord" to Abraham.

Paul remained in his own rented place, on house arrest, with all freedom and without hindrance teaching the things concerning the risen Christ and proclaiming the kingdom of God. And Caesar? Well, it looks like that never happened. Jesus said, "Rome" not Caesar. Paul thought he meant Caesar. They heard what they thought he meant, however, they were closer than we are now. Let's go back and read and meditate on the words of Jesus, the red words, the WORD of God.

Acts 29

OUR LIVES SHOULD BE a continuation of the book of Acts. We are Acts 29 and following. "You are our epistle, having been inscribed in our hearts, being known and being read by all men, it having been made plain that you are Christ's letter, served by us; not having been inscribed by ink but by the Spirit of the living God; not in tables of stone, but in fleshly tablets of the heart" (2 Cor 3:2-3). You have power to love one another as Christ has loved us and power to witness about the resurrection of Jesus. "Going, then, disciple all ethnicities...........".

Printed in the United States
By Bookmasters